"As a somatic psychotherapist, my work with clients often focuses on the debilitating effects of anxiety in their lives. Michele Blume's insightful book provides the missing link between the work I do in the therapy office and the ongoing work clients can continue to do on their own. Through targeted exercises, it provides a road map for those looking to transcend their anxiety and reach their full potential and vitality."

> —**Kelly Mothner, PhD**, psychotherapist in private practice in Hermosa Beach, CA; and certified somatic practitioner (SEP)

"Michele Blume has a deep understanding of the experience of anxiety and how it manifests in the body. Her comprehensive SOAR model offers a road map to healing through the use of relatable case examples, clear and easy-to-follow exercises, and recordings which may be used by clinicians and laypeople alike. As a trauma therapist, I was able to integrate her model into sessions with immediate results. She is a loving guide who exudes compassion, wisdom, knowledge, and humility."

> —**Jenna Abell, PsyD**, trauma and attachment-focused eye movement desensitization and reprocessing (EMDR)-trained psychologist

"In this book, Michele Blume combines her rich clinical experience in implementing mindful somatic awareness with the latest research on the brain, nervous system, and trauma treatment to offer both therapists and clients practical tools and applications for the treatment of anxiety. For psychotherapists who are introducing more and more somatic techniques into their private practice, this book is a must-read. The author shortcuts needless technical jargon, and gets down to what really works to eradicate high-anxiety states."

—**Robert Coffman, PhD**, licensed clinical psychologist
with over forty-five years of clinical experience,
international trainer in bioenergetic analysis; and SEP-,
EMDR-, and Bodynamic-certified

"In this helpful guide, Michele Blume shows that by understanding the origins of your anxiety, you can better mitigate its effects. She knowledgeably walks you through exercises to help you better understand when and how anxiety takes hold of you, offering well-crafted solutions for how to help yourself through the pain of your unique experiences. Blume gently points out that anxiety happens, and that it can often be linked to long-held beliefs from years ago; she then details what you can do about it now. I recommend this book for those suffering from anxiety, and for those looking to help others who are in the throes of their struggle."

—**Rebekkah LaDyne, MS, SEP,**
author of *The Mind-Body Stress Reset*

Mindful Somatic Awareness

for

Anxiety Relief

A body-based approach to
moving beyond fear & worry

Michele L. Blume, PsyD, SEP

New Harbinger Publications, Inc.

Publisher's Note

Distributed in Canada by Raincoast Books

Copyright © 2020 by Michele L. Blume
         New Harbinger Publications, Inc.
         5674 Shattuck Avenue
         Oakland, CA 94609
         www.newharbinger.com

The exercises "Saying No," "Sensing No," and "My Dance Space, Your Dance Space" are adapted from SENSORIMOTOR PSYCHOTHERAPY: INTERVENTIONS FOR TRAUMA AND ATTACHMENT by Pat Ogden and Janina Fischer. Copyright © 2015 by Pat Ogden. Used by permission of W. W. Norton & Company, Inc.

Cover design by Amy Shoup; Acquired by Wendy Millstine;
Edited by Ken Knabb

Library of Congress Cataloging-in-Publication Data

Names: Blume, Michele, author.
Title: Mindful somatic awareness for anxiety relief : a body-based approach to moving beyond fear and worry / by Michele Blume.
Description: Oakland, CA : New Harbinger Publications, [2020] | Includes bibliographical references.
Identifiers: LCCN 2020015020 (print) | LCCN 2020015021 (ebook) | ISBN 9781684035243 (trade paperback) | ISBN 9781684035250 (pdf) | ISBN 9781684035267 (epub)
Subjects: LCSH: Anxiety--Alternative treatment. | Somesthesia. | Mind and body.
Classification: LCC RC531 .B58 2020 (print) | LCC RC531 (ebook) | DDC 616.85/22--dc23
LC record available at https://lccn.loc.gov/2020015020
LC ebook record available at https://lccn.loc.gov/2020015021

Printed in the United States of America

22   21   20

10   9   8   7   6   5   4   3   2   1   First Printing

To Mom and Dad

Contents

Acknowledgments

This book and the ideas in it are strongly influenced by the brilliant work of Dr. Peter Levine and his body-based method for healing trauma, called Somatic Experiencing. Providing both a theoretical framework and a therapeutic technique for understanding and working with trauma and other stress disorders, Somatic Experiencing has forever changed the way I work as a therapist. It has also immeasurably influenced my own healing journey. So I extend my deep gratitude to Dr. Levine as well as to the countless teachers at the Somatic Experiencing Trauma Institute, whose wisdom and guidance have enhanced my understanding of trauma and the body and how to compassionately work with PTSD and the effects of early emotional wounding.

My gratitude also extends to the following teachers, who have profoundly impacted my life and whose energetic imprint permeates the pages of this book. My deepest gratitude goes to Dr. Sally Miller, who taught me the power of loving attunement and the gift of a forgiving heart. With my whole heart I thank Dr. Robert Coffman, who has deepened my understanding of the body's wisdom and its intrinsic capacity to heal; he has taught me the healing power of a secure, loving attachment and continues to show me the transformative power of love. Thank you to my dear friend and brilliant colleague Dr. Kelly Waggoner, whose loving support I could not live without. The levity of your spirit and your ability to see the humor and joy in everything are enviable gifts that inspire my life and work every day. My dear, sweet Nicolas, thank you for showing me the power of devotion and intentional loving. You are the constant rainbow that challenges me to think beyond what my eyes see and to trust what my heart feels. My deep and unending gratitude is due to my clients, past and present, whose courage to engage the healing process inspires me every day. You are among my greatest teachers, and I thank you for entrusting me with the most sacred contents of your hearts and for having faith in my ability to guide your healing. And to Michael and Lorraine Blume, whom I call Mom and Dad: You are my biggest cheerleaders and most ardent fans. Thank you for your faith in me and for trusting the unconventional path I have chosen for my life. Your unconditional love and support have been as constant as the sun and the bedrock of my journey.

Foreword

Anxiety goes beyond our thinking minds. Fear is felt as a swirling in the belly, tension in the chest, sweatiness of the palms, and clenching of the jaw. However, so many therapeutic approaches focus solely on cognitive interventions. We can learn to talk ourselves down from a panic attack, but unless we unpack the underlying experiences that fuel our anxiety, the fear and panic often persist. As a result, we often feel caught in a game of cat and mouse, feeling as though we are constantly being chased, temporarily escaping into freedom, only to replay this process again and again. Dr. Michele Blume reminds us why we cannot think ourselves out of our fear-based responses. Moreover, her somatically based approach will help you learn valuable, body-based exercises to find real, sustained relief.

Our implicit memories play an important role in our sensory-based experiences of fear and anxiety. Implicit memories involve lower brain centers that retain memories of sensations and sequences of movements from the past, including the distant past when we were just little children. Just like learning to ride a bike, once an implicit memory is learned, you no longer need to think about it. Implicit memories carry the felt experience of how we were held, how we felt when we reached out for contact, and whether our feelings were understood when we were children. These implicit memories run in the background of our minds to form the basis of our sense of self and our perceptions of the world around us. Most important, this memory system is resistant to change, unless we learn to access the somatic components of memories.

Many of us have learned to disconnect from the body's natural capacity to sense our environment and to move in response to our world. We might disconnect because of an accumulation of subtle rejections from our parents or as a result of traumatic events. Or we may have learned to override our sensations in order to be a good and obedient student, as stillness is often reinforced in our learning environments. Over time, repeated suppression of our sensory awareness also disconnects us from our emotions. We start to feel "cut off" from ourselves and numb, and it is harder to feel our hurt, anger, sadness, and fear. In this process, however, we also become disconnected from pleasurable emotions such as joy or excitement. While we may have retreated to our thinking minds in order to survive difficult life events, most of us eventually discover that this coping mechanism backfires. In short, we want more out of life.

However, the prospect of reawakening our relationships to our sensations and emotions can initially feel threatening. In many ways we are like a cat stuck high up in a tree. We do not know how to find our way back down to earth. We fear the process of shifting our awareness inward, into the sensate experiences of the body. Throughout the chapters of this book, Dr. Blume guides you to mindfully greet your somatic experience through awareness of sensation, breath, and movement. Recognizing that this process might feel overwhelming, she invites you to pace yourself: to experience sensations slowly and mindfully. For example, in chapter 6, she guides you to develop *dual awareness*, by helping you focus your external awareness on the here and now while building your capacity to attend to sensations, even if they are frightening or uncomfortable.

Most of what we fear is connected to something that has already happened in the past. Our sensations inform our perceptions of what is happening now and can develop into beliefs about what we think will happen in the future. Healing asks us to differentiate between our memories of the past and the possibilities that become available when we start to live fully, in the here and now. What I particularly enjoy about Dr. Blume's approach is the structure that she offers her reader. In short, she creates safety. Within these pages I invite you to sense that you are in the hands of a competent guide, one who has clearly walked this territory of healing herself. Throughout the book you will find invitations to explore yourself and your own embodied experience, and an opportunity to finally find lasting freedom from anxiety.

—Arielle Schwartz
Author of *The Complex PTSD Workbook* (Althea Press, 2016), *EMDR Therapy and Somatic Psychology* (W. W. Norton, 2018), and *The Post-Traumatic Growth Guidebook* (PESI Publishing, 2020).

CHAPTER 1

Anxiety and the Somatic Self

Your body is alive. It is a dynamic organism naturally designed to think, feel, and do, all at the same time—an interplay of phenomena that gives rise to your unique experience of being alive, through which your authentic self finds expression. And it is the unfettered expression of your authentic self that is the wellspring of joy, creativity, happiness, and hope, as well as of courage, determination, resilience, and grace. Anxiety is a clamp that inhibits your impulses to live freely and authentically. It constricts your emotional, physical, and mental mobility, hindering your natural instincts to expand, reach out, connect, and create. Living in fear and worry blocks access to the abundant resources that dwell within you. It douses the inner spark that generates a curious and imaginative approach to living—the approach that accepts and embraces the ever-changing nature of the present moment, allowing you to engage it with an open heart and welcome whatever comes next.

The anguish of living in chronic anticipation of something bad happening is the genuine toll it takes on your physical and emotional well-being. Anxiety inhibits a general sense of ease and pleasure in your day-to-day life. It takes you out of present-moment living, where authentic expression springs eternal, and throws you into the future, where living becomes an exercise in averting crisis or misfortune. Whether it be related to your health, family, work, or finances, you feel certain that something will go wrong and that you will not be effective in preventing or managing it. Further, the corresponding physical effects of anxiety portend apathy and can undermine efforts to engage in your daily responsibilities with a sense of meaning and purpose. Muscle tension, headaches, stomachaches, disturbances in sleeping, eating, breathing, focusing, and mood—all these exhaust your energy, turning life into a list of chores that need to get done.

The effects of anxiety can be far reaching. Anxiety can be the alarm clock that wakes you up in the morning or the mental chatter and restlessness that keeps you up at night. Anxiety can limit the scope of your experiences by inhibiting impulses to play with different ways of seeing your world and move free-spiritedly within it. When your focus is on preventing calamity, it feels too dangerous to take the risks needed to create the life you envision. This holds you back from pursuing desires, manifesting dreams, and even falling in love. Anxiety impacts your relationships, making it difficult to listen attentively, to attune to the needs of others, or to experience emotional comfort and closeness. Always prepared to snuff the flame of spontaneity, anxiety can take the fun and adventure out of life and dash authentic responsiveness to the rich and unique unfolding of the here and now. And sadly, anxiety disconnects you from your intuitive guidance. The innate wisdom of your body that helps light your way becomes tangled with fear and doubt. You are no longer able to align with confidence in the direction of what feels true, whether that be a major life decision, matters of the heart, or your physical health and well-being.

The tragedy of anxiety is the degree to which it can compromise your felt sense of competency, vitality, and resiliency. I have had the honor and privilege of working with some of the most amazing individuals—intelligent, talented, strong, kind, compassionate, loyal, funny, and accomplished. Despite their inherent gifts, it never ceases to amaze me the degree to which their anxiety undermines their felt sense of prowess. I see the way anxiety creates doubt when they consider whether their efforts actually make a difference. It diminishes their ability to engage life with full-bodied enthusiasm and makes it more difficult for them to rebound from adversity. As one of my clients succinctly stated, "Anxiety makes everything hard."

Mary's struggle was no exception. When I first started working with Mary, the effects of anxiety had corroded her spirit. A high-functioning, educated woman who once worked in the corporate sphere, Mary had decided to leave her job after her first child was born, when the unyielding demands of motherhood refused to play nice with the equally unyielding demands of her job. Mary's decision to quit her job was a notable source of anxiety because she was now financially dependent on her husband. This was a reality at odds with her identity as a self-sufficient modern woman and triggered her discomfort in relying on others to meet her needs. Furthermore, with the addition of her second child, Mary's anxiety kicked into high gear as she was run ragged dropping her kids off at school, supervising homework, making dinner, attending dance recitals and PTA meetings, and planning birthday parties. Amid all this, she was doing her best to tend to her marriage, her friendships, and her extended family relationships. Mary also struggled with perfectionism, which was yet another source of her anxiety.

At the outset of my work with Mary, our focus was the cognitive processes that were causing her anxiety. Her anxiety came not only from her infinite to-do list, but also from believing that if everything didn't get done (and get done in a particular way) then some unnamable, awful thing was going to happen. So my goal was to identify Mary's negative thought patterns and change the maladaptive belief systems that influenced her perceptions, emotional reactions, and expectations for how the future would unfold. For example, Mary tended to catastrophize, believing that current situations were worse than they actually were and that future outcomes would unroll with snags and complications that would make demands of her that she could not meet. This would inevitably result in her failing in some way, a reality Mary could not tolerate. Additionally, Mary possessed what we came to call her "Inner Should Monster," a mean-spirited inner voice who made a myriad of demands about how she *should do this,* and how she *should have said that,* or how she *should act this way* and *should never wear that.* All kinds of nonnegotiable rules about life and living and how she *should* conduct herself. Her "Inner Should Monster" not only was a source of anxiety, it left Mary questioning her competency and value as a mother, wife, and friend.

Our efforts to identify and label the cognitive processes that generated and perpetuated Mary's anxiety illuminated important aspects of her thinking that needed to change. However, our efforts were ultimately futile because no amount of cognitive restructuring created lasting relief for Mary. Eventually her compulsive thinking and anxiety would snap back like a rubber band. Only when I went through training in somatic forms of therapeutic interventions did I begin to understand what was really going on with Mary and why her anxiety stubbornly persisted.

Looking at Anxiety Through the Somatic Lens

"Somatic" comes from the Greek word *soma,* which means *living body.* So when we look at anxiety through the somatic lens, we are seeking to understand it with a focus on the body and the intricate neurobiological systems that regulate the continuous stream of internal and external stimuli that inform our present-moment experience. Though a somatic lens focuses on the body, it does not do so to the exclusion of the mind. Rather, it sees the mind as it lives and finds expression in the body. In this way, the somatic lens is holistic and expands the scope of attention and understanding to the whole individual, including both the body *and* the mind, seeing them as a vastly interconnected, dynamically co-arising unit. It emphasizes the unceasing interplay among physical sensation, cognitive processes, and emotional responses to experience that give birth to a felt sense of self in the present moment: Your felt sense of self is a *felt awareness of your experience of yourself, others, and situations; it is the embodiment of an intuitive knowing that emerges from physical sensations and emotional responses* (Gendlin 1978). In addition to fresh, new incoming data from present-moment experience, the neurobiological processes that come together to produce your felt sense are simultaneously being informed by past experiences that are stored in the neural pathways threaded throughout your body. These past experiences are alive in the here and now, actively shaping your thoughts, feelings, perceptions, and behaviors as they emerge with each unfolding moment. In this way, to understand your felt sense of self in the present moment is to also understand your felt sense of self in historical moments.

Our mind-body system is always remembering. This means that recorded in the sweeping expansiveness of your neurobiological systems are *implicit memories* of lived experiences that are actively informing your perceptions, and therefore your interpretation of current and future events and circumstances. Implicit memories are not recalled as a conscious flow of specific, detailed information about an event that happened once upon a time. Rather, implicit memories are unconscious bits and pieces of unaltered sensory data encoded with the thoughts and emotions they had at the moment they were experienced. Moreover, implicit memories are not experienced as something that happened in the past, but as something that is happening right here, right now. They carry with them the immediacy of the present moment, and when the emotional charge of the implicit memory is high, they can make the past indistinguishable from the present. When we consider anxiety in light of implicit body memory, we consider the various streams of incoming information from past and present that give meaning to your perceptions in the here and now and ask the question: *What is causing your mind-body to believe that something bad is going to happen? What is causing you to be afraid?*

Understanding anxiety through the somatic lens, then, is to see that *anxiety is a state of present-moment fear based on past experiences that are informing your expectations of future events.* Moreover, anxiety includes the fear that the expected bad thing will exceed or overwhelm your ability to successfully prevent or manage it and that it will ultimately compromise your life in some unforeseeable way. Anxiety keeps your mind hypervigilant in its expectation that adverse events will happen and keeps your body primed to mobilize in response to such adverse events. The shift in perspective the somatic lens offers is that the origin of anxiety is encoded in somatic or implicit memory. This means that at some point in your past, you felt frightened or overwhelmed by certain events or circumstances where you could not respond in a way that ensured your emotional or physical feeling of safety, security, or empowerment. These experiences were recorded in your unconscious somatic memory system and are now being recalled to interpret the present and future in such a way that will ensure that, this time, you will emerge triumphant should the bad thing happen again. So now the question becomes: *What historical experience is my body remembering that has me fearful that something will go wrong or something bad will happen? And why do I believe I will not be able to successfully confront this bad thing?*

As we explore the answers to these questions in the upcoming chapters, it is important to remember that anything that overwhelms your physiological or emotional ability to respond can be considered something frightening and disempowering. These fear-based experiences do not have to be major traumatic events, and often they aren't. This is what makes these questions so hard to answer. Further, many of the events that compromised your felt sense of emotional or physical safety and security likely happened during your childhood, when your ability to understand and respond to the world was facilitated by a developing brain with fledgling logic. In fact, as young children, our neurobiological development is such that our way of experiencing and making sense of our surroundings is predominantly sensory and emotional. Our reasoning ability lags way behind. These inherent conditions of young life can make the experience of being a child very difficult and scary at times, even in the best of circumstances. It is also important to note that the memory systems most active during childhood are predominantly implicit. This means that much of the biographical data recorded in your implicit memories, which actively inform your interpretation of present-day experience, actually came from your childhood.

When we reflect on our experiences as a child, we often reflect on them with the mind of an adult and therefore use adult reasoning to consider how those experiences may have impacted us. But when you were a child, you did not have an adult mind. What seems like an innocuous event now may have been overwhelming for you as a child. Keep this in mind as you engage in the exercises in this book and begin to understand what it is you are fearful of and how it gives rise to your anxiety.

I will return to Mary's story to bring to life the power of early encoding of implicit memory and its ability to generate anxiety. We know that Mary tended to catastrophize circumstances and that she struggled with fears of dependency and failure. She didn't like asking for help and insisted on doing everything herself. She also insisted on doing everything perfectly. Why would Mary feel this way? Where do these fears, beliefs, and behavior patterns come from?

Mary's life is shaped by a myriad of important experiences. However, we can turn our focus specifically toward Mary's childhood and her parents' divorce. Though it wasn't a particularly bitter divorce, the rupture of her family unit naturally rattled Mary's sense of security and stability. She was a young girl whose secure base and safe place was now fractured and uncertain. What's more, the divorce created financial strain for Mary's mother, with whom she spent most of her time. According to Mary, the financial stress was palpable, and Mary could feel the tension of her mother's worry when she came home from school and saw her mother crunching numbers at the kitchen table. She could see the financial hardship in her mother's dispirited posture and hear it in her heavy sighs as she sifted through bills and receipts. This worried young Mary considerably, making her fearful not only for their future stability, but of placing additional demands on her mother lest she burden her even more. To offset her mother's stress as well as to ease her own feelings of powerlessness, Mary became more self-sufficient, making her own lunch for school and doing her own laundry. She even added extra chores to her list in the hopes it would further alleviate her mother's stress and fatigue.

Mary's mother was a very kind and nurturing presence who never openly complained about money or made her feel like a burden. And yet Mary nonetheless emerged from this time in her life fearful of financial scarcity, of being a burden, and of being dependent on others. The experience of her parents' divorce was overwhelming for young Mary. She felt frightened, vulnerable, and powerless. To relieve these often intolerable feelings, at a young age Mary decided she would never be dependent on anyone—she would make her own money and take care of her own needs. Though Mary's worst fears never came true, they were still unconsciously wired into the neural pathways of her somatic self. Her old fears now inform her current thought processes and perceptions, causing her significant anxiety.

Neurobiology 101

As we peer into past experiences recorded in the deeper folds of your somatic self to examine the source of your anxiety, it is helpful to have a basic understanding of how the mind and body work together to respond and adapt to your surroundings. It is also important to see how these responses are recorded in implicit memory and then used to inform present-moment experience. This will acquaint you with the unique interplay of the physiological, emotional, and cognitive processes that generate your anxiety so that you can use the exercises in the upcoming chapters to develop the skills to mitigate it.

What follows is a brief illustration of the cooperative efforts of the brain and the nervous system to respond and adapt to the continuous shifts in the conditions of your internal and external environment. This working relationship facilitates your felt sense of self in each moment, giving rise to your unique experience as a thinking, feeling being. In this chapter, I'll describe the different parts separately to best illuminate their distinct functions. However, it is important to remember they are a collaboration of parts operating as a whole system—parts that together give color and texture to your subjective experience of being alive.

The Autonomic Nervous System

The autonomic nervous system (ANS) is an acutely sensitive and highly attuned network of neural pathways woven throughout your body. It is designed to actively respond and adapt to your ever-changing felt sense of the world around you. Operating largely without your conscious awareness, it regulates the vital life-sustaining processes of your body, such as respiration and heart rate, as well as the activity of your internal organs. When the ANS detects any threat or danger in your environment, real or perceived, it instinctively and instantly responds, facilitating a cascade of internal processes to prepare your body for protective action and ensure your survival.

The ANS is a complex system with three separate divisions. However, for our purposes here, we will focus on only two of these divisions: the sympathetic nervous system and the parasympathetic nervous system.

The Sympathetic Nervous System

The sympathetic nervous system (SNS) regulates internal states of arousal and is commonly known for mobilizing the fight-or-flight defense. When the body's threat-detecting system perceives danger, it increases the activity of the SNS, which prepares the body for action by initiating physiological changes such as increased heart rate, blood pressure, and respiration. When the threat is removed, the SNS downregulates to help restore physiological equilibrium. Anxiety, however, keeps the SNS chronically activated. This means that when you are feeling anxious, you are acutely sensitive to environmental triggers, and your body is primed to mobilize in response to those triggers. Have you ever noticed that when you are anxious, the littlest thing can set you off, generating anger, irritability, or such a feeling of being overwhelmed that you want to throw your hands up in the air? This is because when that little thing happened, your body was already in a state of sympathetic arousal and the new trigger just intensified the activation beyond what feels comfortable and what seems reasonable.

The Parasympathetic Nervous System

The parasympathetic nervous system (PNS) is known as the "rest and digest" system. It is the branch of the ANS that helps you release muscle tension, lowers your heart rate and blood pressure, and aids your digestion. Mindfulness and relaxation exercises all target the PNS to bring the body into a state of calm. In this way, the PNS helps facilitate physiological recovery from sympathetic activation. However, the PNS also aids in protecting you from danger. When the body experiences serious threat and is in a state of extreme SNS arousal but the fight-or-flight response is ineffective or not possible, the PNS will override SNS activation to immobilize the body. In other words, the PNS can veto an SNS response and shut the body down. This is known as a *freeze* response. Have you ever experienced a situation where you were so overwhelmed that your mind "went blank" and you couldn't think? Or you "clammed up" and couldn't speak? Or you "froze" and couldn't move? These are all examples of the PNS initiating a freeze response by shutting down SNS activation. Though these experiences are incredibly frustrating and can even worsen anxiety, they are actually intended to ensure your survival.

A true partnership, the sympathetic and parasympathetic nervous systems join forces to help your body respond and adjust to the ongoing environmental changes happening within and around you. With your safety and protection as their primary concern, the neural pathways of the SNS and PNS are forever scanning the environment for cues to ensure your survival. Because the physiological shifts generated by ANS activation can instantly change your felt sense and trigger your anxiety, cultivating awareness of these often subtle somatic changes can help you stabilize ANS activation before it recruits other neural systems to facilitate a heightened fear response. Fine-tuning your felt-sense awareness also invites you to explore your implicit memories by learning to identify the triggers that caused the fear response and to understand why you experience those triggers as dangerous or threatening.

In addition to its role in regulating life-sustaining and life-protecting processes, the ANS is also intimately involved in neural processing. What follows is a brief exploration of the different regions of the brain, how they function together, and how they process information communicated by the ANS.

The Brain: One Country, Three Regions

An incredibly complex organ, the brain is continuously being shaped and reshaped by your ongoing experiences. Your very own neurobiological computer stationed right inside your skull, the brain contains about one billion neurons, all interconnected and capable of transmitting information at a speed of over 200 miles per hour (Siegel 2010). Further, the brain is receiving, processing, and transmitting information every single moment of every single day. When you consider the vast interconnectedness of all the neurons in the brain and its capacity to instantly transmit massive amounts of information to every organ, muscle, and tissue in the body, you can begin to see how powerful it is in its ability to initiate various states of activation and alter your felt sense in any given moment. In light of this, a key component to regulating your fear response and achieving anxiety relief is knowing your body-brain and the way it responds to environmental triggers. This will help you understand the source of your anxiety activation as well as your patterns of anxiety activation so you can bring your body back into a state of regulation.

What follows is an illustration of the basic functions of this miraculous structure in order to highlight the ways in which it can generate and perpetuate anxiety. The brain is often divided into three regions: the brain stem, the limbic region, and the neocortex, with each region serving a particular function. Though these regions each have a specialized function, they are designed to work together to maintain equilibrium amid ever-changing internal and external conditions.

The Brain Stem

The brain stem is located at the back of your brain and sits right atop the spine. The structures of the brain stem form the hub of the autonomic regulatory processes that communicate with your body to control basic life-sustaining functions such as heart rate, respiration, and temperature. As the heart of autonomic activity, the brain stem also participates in mobilizing your body's instinctive survival responses in times of danger. Additionally, the brain stem facilitates motor control and coordinates the refinement of movement and balance, allowing us to move with ease and grace as we engage in physical activities. So we can thank the brain stem not only for its life-saving attributes, but also for our ability to dance a waltz, ride a bike, and balance on a tightrope. The many neurophysiological functions of the brain stem reflect its participation in somatosensory experience and its leading role in giving you a felt sense in each unfolding moment.

The brain stem receives a virtually infinite stream of information from the body and then filters it before sending it upstream to higher cortical areas, where the information is evaluated for its usefulness and then processed accordingly. The directional flow of incoming information enables the brain stem to imbue the data sent upward with a felt-sense experience, which then influences thoughts, feelings, perceptions, and behaviors (Badenoch 2018). In other words, the brain stem helps facilitate your felt sense of self as you engage with others and the world around you. It also archives your felt experience in implicit memory. However, when the information first reaches the brain stem, it is sensory in nature. Not until it reaches the limbic region and neocortex is the information given emotional and cognitive meaning.

The Limbic Region

The limbic region is located in the heart of the brain, sitting above the brain stem and below the neocortex. This region is often referred to as the emotion center of the brain because of its role in regulating your emotional responses to the world around you and your relationships within it. Composed of several structures, such as the amygdala and the hippocampus, the limbic region evaluates the emotional significance of your experiences and decides if they are meaningful to you. In doing so, it helps weave together the colorful tapestry of your emotional life through which your felt sense finds expression. In keeping with the vast interconnectedness of neurobiological processes, the limbic region is in constant communication with other brain structures, including the insula, which connects emotional meaning to body sensation and behavior (Namkung, Kim, and Sawa 2017; Levine 2010). The neural conversation among these brain regions creates an emotional context for your felt-sense experience and the behavioral impulses that emerge from it (Damasio, Damasio, and Tranel 2012). When we consider the emotion-regulating function of the limbic system and its relationship with the insula and other brain regions, we can begin to think about how limbic activity plays a key role in generating anxiety and how implicit memory triggers a fear response.

The limbic system is continually evaluating and processing incoming information. With rapid precision, it attaches emotional significance to neural data and sends it off to other brain centers for further evaluation. However, when assessing novel information to determine emotional significance, the limbic system also consults implicit body memory. If the sensory conditions of the present moment, such as sight, smell, taste, and even the feel of your skin, resemble the events of the past and carry with them a similar emotional quality, then the neural evaluation of this information will be that the situations are likely the same—and if the situations are the same, then they require the same response. Further, if the emotional intensity of the implicit memory is high, then the limbic process, with the help of the brain stem, will hijack a higher, more logical assessment from more analytical parts of your brain—an assessment that could prevent a reactive response. When this happens, it will inhibit your ability to distinguish the past from the present, causing you to respond to the present as if it were the past. When we consider limbic activity in light of anxiety, we can see how unresolved past experiences of being afraid and overwhelmed impact present-moment perceptions and behaviors.

Remember, implicit memory of unresolved fear-based experiences from the past contain fragments of the historical experience that are encoded with the sensory data, emotional responses, thought processes, and behavioral impulses you had during that time. Coming to know the unique way your emotional experiences have been inscribed in your somatic memory system is an important part of understanding the origins of your anxiety and taking steps to relieve it. In the chapters to come, I'll provide you with exercises to help you connect to the sensory memories at the heart of your anxiety as well as to the fear-based thoughts, beliefs, and behaviors linked to them. Identifying your fear-based sensory memories and their corresponding cognitive processes will help you understand the unconscious ways you made sense of the experience at the time. In doing so, it will bring to light the origins of your anxiety and the measures needed to relieve it.

In addition to the unconscious ways our brain makes sense of our experiences, there are also conscious ways it creates meaning. These processes are controlled by the neocortex.

The Neocortex

Spread across the top of your head and behind your forehead, the neocortex is the region of the brain that facilitates cognitive processes such as reasoning, abstraction, problem solving, and planning. The neural circuits in this region give rise to insight and ideas; they attach meaning to your experiences, and they help you plan and make decisions about the future. In keeping with the brain's complexity, the neocortex is divided vertically into two hemispheres— the right and the left hemisphere—with neural circuits in both hemispheres firing for every experience. The two hemispheres are designed to dance in sync with one another, integrating their distinct cognitive rhythms and styles to create a three-dimensional flow and groove to your thought processes and perceptions. However, within the neural folds of an anxious mind, the right and left hemispheres tend to dance out of step and clash in their efforts to coordinate movement into a rhythmic flow.

THE RIGHT HEMISPHERE

Oriented toward your emotional, relational, and felt-sense experience, the neural pathways of the right hemisphere process the often subtle and nonverbal subtext of your surroundings and the people in them. Using nonlinear, intuitive logic, the right hemisphere attunes predominantly to the present moment, with specific focus on how this moment feels and how this feeling is meaningful to you. The lens of the right hemisphere is curious and holistic, seeing your world as composed of parts linked together to create a whole subjective experience fused with the unique attributes of your personality. It makes sense, then, that the right hemisphere is also more directly influenced by the lower regions of the brain, such as the limbic system and brain stem, which unconsciously mediate emotional responses, bodily functions, and survival instincts. This enables the right hemisphere to use somatic, implicit data to inform its cognitive processing. In this way, the right hemisphere carries the truth of your subjective experience as it is felt throughout your body and informs its perceptions with this deeper felt-sense way of knowing.

THE LEFT HEMISPHERE

The neural processes of the left hemisphere could not be more different from those of the right. While the right brain is concerned with the feeling and deeper meaning of your experiences, the left brain is literal and practical in its perspective. The lens of the left hemisphere is analytical and sees things with the intention of breaking them into parts and analyzing each one for its functional relevance. The left brain is very logical and orderly, using linear thought processes and reason to understand and make sense of your world. While the right hemisphere understands and can tolerate the uncertainty of the present moment, the left hemisphere prefers constancy, predictability, and stability. It thus tends to be very discerning and judgmental, and often implements rules and regulations for correct ways of seeing and doing. It does this with the intention of maintaining order in your internal and external environments. With all of this, it makes sense that most of our language abilities are wired into the left hemisphere, creating swift access to the skills needed to clearly verbalize the neat and tidy ways it sees and expects things to be.

When they function together, the right and left hemispheres integrate logical and intuitive information, allowing you to form a more dynamic experience of life and living that is organized and reasoned as well as rich with an emotional felt sense. The collaborative partnership of the two hemispheres enables you to collect intuitive as well as practical information from your experiences, to analyze it, to develop insights, and to attach meaning to it. This combined effort creates context for here-and-now subjective experiences and enables you to cast your sights forward and plan for the future. However, when the left and right hemispheres are at odds with one another, or if one hemisphere dominates cognitive processing to the near exclusion of the other, the communication disruption can often reflect something deeper going on, such as unresolved fears. For example, when the mind-body is anxious, the right hemisphere can overwhelm the more rational left hemisphere. The left hemisphere may then respond to this by trying to disconnect from the more emotional right hemisphere in order to preserve its functional integrity. However, when unresolved fear is worked through and the nervous system is regulated, the right and left hemispheres can effectively collaborate to weave together rational thought with intuitive knowing, creating an embodied present-moment experience.

Tying the Threads Together: The Brain and Anxiety

In a well-functioning neurobiological system, the ANS and all three regions of the brain communicate to respond efficiently and effectively to fluctuations in the external environment and to maintain smooth and balanced regulation of your internal environment. Problems arise when implicit memory systems—which, again, encode memories in the neural pathways of your body that inform your thoughts, beliefs, perceptions, and behaviors in each moment—contain unknown and unresolved fears. When activated, these implicit memory systems trigger a fear response, and this fear response often hijacks higher cognitive processes that would help you interpret circumstances with logic and reason.

When the brain and nervous system are communicating coherently, the information offered by implicit memory systems doesn't determine outcome, but is combined with the logical thought processes of the left hemisphere to create an integrated perspective. Put differently, when all the parts of your neurobiological system are collaborating with ease and communication is fluid, then your interpretation of, and therefore your response to, your environment is one that balances logical reasoning and felt-sense knowing. This gives rise to a grounded present-moment experience. Unfortunately for those who suffer from persistent anxiety, the neurobiological system can be dis-integrated, with particular parts of it becoming too reactive and overwhelming to others. The system then struggles to collaborate in a way that enables us to see situations clearly and accurately, especially when strong implicit memories come into play.

Let's return to Mary to see just how this works. As a child, Mary felt overwhelmed and frightened when her parents divorced. The felt experience of this fear wove itself into her implicit memory system and, unbeknownst to her, became activated when she found herself in a state of dependency again after quitting her job. Unconsciously, Mary was interpreting her present experience of dependency as being the same or similar to her childhood experience of dependency, triggering all her old fears. As a result, her brain stem, limbic system, and the right hemisphere of her neocortex—all carriers of implicit memory—mobilized a fear response which settled into a chronic state of anxiety. To alleviate her anxiety, Mary's left hemisphere went into overdrive. For example, Mary's "Inner Should Monster," whose purpose it was to enforce systematic rules for how things *should* be done in order to maintain predictability and stability, reflected her attempt to override implicit memory activation. This would alleviate her fear and create a felt sense of security. In this way, Mary's overactive thinking not only helped her feel in control, it also took her out of the bad feelings, which were sometimes intolerable. Mary's "Inner Should Monster" was trying to preserve the integrity of her somatic self so that her fear did not overwhelm her and she could go about her day. Ultimately, however, it made her anxiety worse.

It wasn't until I incorporated somatic therapeutic exercises into her therapy that Mary's anxiety began to diminish. By turning our focus to the somatic sensations Mary would experience as she told her story, she was able to move into a deeper understanding of the fear that lived in her body and work through it. This was because encoded in those sensations was the subjective truth of Mary's experience *as it was previously experienced,* not as it was understood by her adult mind. When we tended to her somatic, implicit memory, it was like going back in time to be with young Mary, back when she was a scared little girl, so that we could give her the reassurance now that she never got then, so that we could quiet her fears and let her know that everything would be okay.

Looking through the somatic lens, we can now see how the source of persistent anxiety is found in unconscious implicit memory. However, now that you know this, how can you access unconscious information that can help you regulate your nervous system and mitigate your anxiety? In the chapters that follow, I will teach you exactly that. Unconscious implicit memory is somatic in nature. That is, it lives in the body. So we will turn our attention to your felt-sense experience in order to find the portal to the unconscious thoughts and beliefs that influence your perceptions and cause your anxiety. The upcoming pages highlight various sources of anxiety common to everyone and provide you with exercises to cultivate Mindful Somatic Awareness. These exercises will help connect you to your body's innate ability to heal the emotional wounds at the core of your fear and chronic worry and help you achieve lasting relief from anxiety.

There are also several related guided meditations that you can access at the website for this book: http://www.newharbinger.com /45243. (See the very back of this book for more details.)

CHAPTER 2

Mindful Somatic Awareness

The journey inward to explore your implicit memory isn't always easy, but it is always rewarding. Hidden in the mysterious landscape of the unconscious emotional life that dwells in your body is a virtual treasure trove of information to help you understand your experience of the present moment and how to navigate it. Your body is rich with wisdom that can guide you toward healing the unresolved fears that trigger your anxiety. Your job is simply to learn how to listen to the voice of your body and translate what you hear it saying. The ability to attune to your body's unique voice and understand what it is telling you is an essential component of anxiety relief that I call *Mindful Somatic Awareness.*

In this chapter, I will help you cultivate the skill of Mindful Somatic Awareness so that you can fine-tune your ability to recognize your body's distinct anxiety cues and listen to what they are telling you about your present-moment experience as well as your perceptions of the future. This will help you settle your reactions before they escalate into a heightened fear response. It will also help facilitate healing of the deeper wounds linked with the unresolved fears at the core of your anxiety.

What Is Mindful Somatic Awareness?

Mindful Somatic Awareness is the ability to listen to the unique voice of your body, understand the information it is communicating to you, and use this information to quiet your anxiety. It requires deliberate effort to resist reacting to your fear-based perceptions and to shift your attention to the sensations activated in your body—the sensations that give rise to your felt sense. Further, it requires nonjudgmental acceptance of the felt-sense awareness you are experiencing and an effort to reflect and understand the information embedded in this new felt-sense awareness.

When we become aware of our body sensations, we often form opinions about them or judge them to decide if they are good or bad. This distances us from our sensations and prevents us from accessing their deeper meaning. Mindful Somatic Awareness requires that you resist the impulse to judge your sensations and instead simply observe them as they arise. Once you are aware of your sensations and the various ways they are vibrating in your body, you can begin to reflect on the felt-sense experience that emerges. This process of observing present-moment sensory experience coupled with contemplative reflection connects you to the deeper meaning carried in your felt sense. And as you connect to the implicit meaning of your felt sense experience, you have access to important information to help guide *mindful action*—choices to act that are grounded in present-moment awareness and informed by both intuitive knowing (right hemisphere) and logical thinking (left hemisphere).

The intention behind Mindful Somatic Awareness is not to sit with and steep in uncomfortable body sensations. Rather, it is to sit with your sensations long enough to give them an opportunity to reveal the deeper message they carry about the implicit memory that has been activated. This can reveal the historical origins of your fear response, as well as provide you with an intuitive knowing of what steps you need to take to bring yourself back into a state of regulation. These steps may be practical, like talking to someone about a particular issue that is concerning you, or they may be more intro-spective, such as journaling or meditating. Either way, they are responses that are rooted in an instinctive felt sense of what you need, not a reactive response to what you *think* you need. In being patient with your felt sense, you are allowing your sensations to organically guide you toward authentic responsiveness to the here and now, which naturally relieves anxiety.

How Mindful Somatic Awareness Helps Reduce Your Anxiety

When we are seized with anxiety, our behavior tends to become reactive because we cannot tolerate the way fear feels in our body—it is a very uncomfortable and sometimes unbearable emotion to experience. So, naturally, we do things to try to alleviate it. Sometimes our efforts to alleviate our fear can be helpful—for example, when we reach out to a friend, go for a walk, or journal our thoughts and feelings. However, sometimes our attempts to allevi-ate fear can be harmful; they can be reactive, feel compulsive, and harden into fixed and unyielding routines. When this happens, our efforts to relieve our fear become problematic and end up making our anxiety worse.

When you are in a reactive mode of responding to fear, the dis-tinction between thoughts of fear and feelings of fear becomes blurred. In other words, *you become your fear,* a mind-body state that then governs your thoughts and perceptions, keeping you in a state of anxiety. But when you pause and intentionally shift your nonjudg-mental attention to your sensations and then reflect on them to understand them, you create distance between your thoughts of fear and feelings of fear. Differentiating your thoughts and feelings helps you to see that *you are not your fear.* Rather, *you are simply experiencing fear.* With this shift in attention, you uncouple yourself from the fear and become the awareness behind it. This process naturally reduces activity in the fear-generating parts of your brain and organically downregulates anxiety (Ogden and Fisher 2015). It also enables you to observe your felt-sense reaction to the present moment, to understand this reaction, and then to integrate this understanding into mindful action. Put differently, Mindful Somatic Awareness facilitates integration of the right and left hemispheres, combining rational thought with felt-sense knowing, enabling you to make reasoned, nonreactive decisions.

Although Mindful Somatic Awareness can help provide immediate relief from anxiety, its true gift is in its potential to help you achieve lasting relief from your anxiety. It does this by helping you heal the original fears that cause it. As I mentioned, Mindful Somatic Awareness gives you access to unconscious implicit memory. More specifically, it connects you to the implicit memory that contains fragments of the behavioral impulses, physical sensations, and emotional responses you had during the original frightening or overwhelming experience—the experience (or experiences) at the root of your anxiety. If you are able to patiently attune to your felt sense and observe your sensations without reacting to them, they will connect to deeper neural processes that eventually reveal more clearly the historical nature of your fear response. This information is not revealed to your conscious mind as a clear and explicit picture of what happened. Rather, the information arrives as a felt-sense knowing, like a deep resonance in your body or a gut feeling you suddenly have about the truth of what you lived through and the impact this deeply emotional experience had on you.

When this felt sense comes in, it gives you a very strong somatic awareness of why you felt overwhelmed or frightened. Further, the emerging felt sense has the potential to release powerful emotions connected to the triggering memory. For example, you may experience fear and begin to tremble. Or you may feel grief or sadness and begin to cry. You may also experience a release of emotion that compels you to reach out to a friend or loved one for comfort. These instinctive responses may surprise you because they may feel new and unfamiliar and they may not be ways you would ordinarily sooth your emotional self. Nevertheless, I encourage you to allow their unfolding, because they echo the wisdom of your body directing you toward what you need to do to resolve old fear and relieve your anxiety.

When you give way to your body's instincts and allow your body to discharge the emotional energy it has been carrying, you may also experience a subtle but powerful physiological shift. This shift is the release of tension held in your body, a relief that gives rise to feelings of lightness and relief. It also opens your somatic self to experience new, more pleasurable sensations, such as relaxation, levity, and joy. Additionally, when the body is no longer constricted with anxiety, it may instinctively orient toward a practical solution, whether addressing real problems in the present moment or planning for future events. Here, mindful action can emerge to help you. This process contributes not only to a sense of relief, but also to one of personal empowerment. When you sit in Mindful Somatic Awareness, you become alive to yourself in a whole new way. You come into an awareness of what you survived and a deep appreciation for how incredibly adaptive and resilient you are. You realize all the internal resources available to you and that you are, in fact, potent and capable of having a profound impact on your environment and the people within it.

Mindful Somatic Awareness in Action

Let's return to Mary (from chapter 1) to demonstrate the power of Mindful Somatic Awareness and its potential to help heal the fears at the core of your anxiety. To recap, Mary struggled with fears of financial scarcity, of dependency, and of being a burden. She also held herself to an unattainable standard of perfection and did not like asking for help. Although Mary was cognitively aware of these fears and where they came from, her body nonetheless continued to hold onto them—they remained wired in her somatic, implicit memory and therefore continued to serve as a notable source of her anxiety.

One day in session, while Mary was reflecting on the way her anxiety was linked to the circumstances of her parent's divorce, I noticed that her breath appeared shallow, her feet were restless, and her hands were clasped. I asked her to pause for a moment and bring her attention to the sensations she felt in her body to see if she might notice how her body was actively demonstrating a fear response. At first, Mary didn't quite understand what I meant. So I explained that her body was listening to her tell her story and it was letting us know that the story made it feel afraid. If we paused long enough and attuned to her felt sense, it might share with us its own version of how it experienced the circumstances of her young life and why it still carried this fear.

To help orient Mary toward her internal body sensations, I guided her attention to her breath. When she focused on her breath, she noticed not only that it was shallow but that her chest felt heavy, "like something was sitting on it." I asked her to hang out with that sensation for a little while to see if it changed, or if she became aware of other body sensations. After a few moments, she looked down at her belly and said she felt a "knot" in her stomach. I asked her to describe the knot, if she could. What did it look like? How big was it? Did it have a color? Often when we experience a sensation, an image of what that sensation looks like might come to mind. It is helpful to describe such a sensation because it facilitates the process of connecting to implicit memory and maintains connection to somatic awareness (Levine 2005). It also helps contain the sensations, so they don't feel overwhelming.

As Mary tended to the sensation in her belly, she noted that the knot was "blue" and looked like a boating knot, an awareness she quickly associated with her father, who loved to sail. As Mary continued to focus on the knot in her stomach, she noticed a new sensation. She described what felt like a wave of energy moving upward in her chest toward her throat. I asked her to follow the movement of that energy, if she could. As Mary tracked that sensation, she suddenly gasped and took a big breath. As she exhaled, her whole body collapsed and she began to cry. I sat with Mary as she wept. After a few moments, through her tears, she quietly whispered, "I missed him so much. I forgot how much I missed my father after the divorce, when I was living with my mom."

Sitting in Mindful Somatic Awareness, Mary reflected on the implicit memories that began to come forward—memories her body had been carrying since her childhood. She recalled that although she saw her father regularly, she missed his presence in the house. She experienced him as strong and capable, someone who made her feel that everything was going to be okay. She noted that she never realized how much of her fear was connected to the absence of his reassuring presence. With this awareness came additional sensations and corresponding recollections. For example, Mary remembered lying in bed at night, fighting the impulse to get up and ask her mother if they had enough money. But because she feared the truth of what her mother might say, she decided instead to be proactive.

She decided to help save money by cutting coupons and not asking for new clothes or school supplies. As Mary sat in contemplation of all the old feelings and memories emerging, she began to see that she coped with her fears by holding everything inside and becoming self-sufficient and independent.

Through the lens of her somatic self, Mary also began to see connections between her past and present. She noted how her new dependency on her husband triggered all these old fears and her response to them was exactly the same as it was when she was a child—to hold her feelings inside, cut off any felt sense of need, and do everything herself. However, what also emerged with this new somatic awareness was the realization of what Mary needed to do now to quell her anxiety. The mindful action she needed to take was something she had wanted to do as a child, but was too afraid to do—she needed to share her fears and seek comfort and reassurance from those who loved her, such as her husband. In order to ease her anxiety, she had to include him in her process so that he could provide emotional and practical support. Mary needed to take a risk and allow her heart to open up to her husband so she could experience in him the warm, reassuring embrace she had longed for as a child.

Until now, Mary had assumed that her fears would burden her husband, much like she had once assumed they would burden her mother. But as she released old emotional energy from her body, she connected to what she knew to be true—her husband did not scare easily and was capable of handling big feelings. Moreover, not only would he want to know these things so that he could help, he would feel awful knowing she had been suffering in solitude. Mary's old fears kept her from seeing this, and therefore kept her from knowing that this was what she needed in order to feel safe, secure, and empowered. As she oriented toward a practical solution, she felt relief in knowing that she no longer had to suffer alone, as she had done when she was young. Rather, she could have a reliable partner in her husband as she adapted to these new frightening changes in her life.

Now that you have a general understanding of Mindful Somatic Awareness, it's time to shift gears and begin the process of cultivating this skill so you can use it to reduce your own anxiety and resolve the fears that cause it. As we begin, it is important to keep in mind that, like any skill, Mindful Somatic Awareness takes intentional effort and practice to develop. In the beginning it may not always feel comfortable or natural. You may wonder, *Am I doing this right?* I encourage you to stay with it. Your body is innately designed to strive for health and wellness; it instinctively knows how to heal itself. In every breathing moment, without your conscious direction, the neural pathways of your body are working to integrate mind-body processes in order to maintain the integrity of your physical, emotional, and psychological self. When you employ Mindful Somatic Awareness, you give your body the chance to organically move out of fear and into a state of regulation.

Cultivating Mindful Somatic Awareness with SOAR

Cultivating the skill of Mindful Somatic Awareness is something anyone can do. It is easiest to do when your nervous system is in a state of relative calmness and you can focus with greater ease. Implementing Mindful Somatic Awareness when your anxiety is heightened may be more challenging. It is during these moments that your impulse to reactively alleviate your fear is strongest. To help you cultivate the skill of Mindful Somatic Awareness and increase your success in using it during times of increased anxiety, I have created an easy-to-use acronym: SOAR.

SOAR stands for sense, observe, articulate, reflect. By *sensing* your body, *observing* what you sense, *articulating* what you observe, and *reflecting* on what you articulate, you can integrate right and left hemisphere functioning to regulate your nervous system and cultivate Mindful Somatic Awareness.

The benefits of SOAR are many. For one, it swiftly targets your parasympathetic nervous system, helping to bring your body back into a state of regulation. It also facilitates connection to your implicit body memory, generating a felt-sense experience that can yield more nuanced information about your anxiety. When combined with explicit awareness, this implicit information creates a more coherent and cohesive understanding of the unresolved fears at the core of your anxiety. And as the deeper dynamics of your anxiety come into view, you can begin to identify your anxiety triggers as well as the emotional reactions, thought patterns, and behavior responses associated with them. This, in turn, creates the opportunity to respond differently to your anxiety triggers, and over time this new way of responding can create a lasting change in your fear-response patterns. Additionally, the felt sense that emerges when you SOAR has the potential to release a range of emotions connected to your implicit memory—emotions such as fear, sadness, anger, disappointment, and hurt. The release of these emotions coupled with new insight helps regulate your nervous system and orients you in the direction of what your mind-body needs to heal the emotional wounds at the core of your anxiety.

The backdrop of SOAR is the integration of your right and left hemispheres—you turn first to your body for information and then use your logic and reason to help you understand that information. Through *sensing* and *observing*, you connect to the intuitive felt-sense awareness of your right hemisphere. And through *articulation* and *reflection*, you engage the more logical abilities of the left hemisphere. Through this process, SOAR promotes neural integration of both hemispheres, giving you the somatic *and* cognitive keys to relieving anxiety, fear, and worry. The collaboration of right and left hemisphere functioning enables mindful action, allowing you to engage the present moment in a more grounded and open-hearted way.

Let's look at each part of the SOAR process in turn and see how you can use it to enhance Mindful Somatic Awareness.

Sense

To sense is to turn your attention to your somatic self and become aware of the sensations in your body. Sensing means to connect to the energy in your nervous system and experience the unique way it is vibrating. To sense is to actively notice physical sensations such as muscle tension, shallow breath, tingling in your legs, or butterflies in your stomach. It is to notice if your head feels heavy, if your shoulders want to collapse, if your face feels flushed, or if you have a lump in your throat. When you tune in and focus on your body sensations, they tend to amplify, which makes them easier to notice. They also tend to move and change, as if your attention gives them permission to come to life in new ways. At first, connecting to your body and sensing its energetic movement may be difficult. It may take some time for sensations to come online, so to speak—we can think so much faster than we can feel. But be patient. So long as your body is alive with energy, it will seek to express this energy through sensation.

The following exercise will help enhance your ability to attune to your somatic self and foster awareness of the sensations that vibrate in your body.

Pause and Sense

Find a quiet place where you will not be distracted. Take off your shoes and sit with your feet flat against the ground. Once you feel settled, close your eyes and bring your attention to your breath. Take three deep breaths, inhaling through your nose and exhaling through your mouth. Next, think of something that gives you a feeling of comfort and safety. For example, a friend, a pet, or a place in nature that you love. Hold this in mind for a minute or two. Now bring your attention back to your breath. What do you notice? Did it change? Did it relax or deepen? Did it constrict? As you notice your breath, gradually broaden your attention to your body and the sensations you are experiencing. What do you notice? What physical sensations are you aware of? Is there a part of your body that feels relaxed? If so, what part? Do you notice any tingling or warmth? If so, where? Are you experiencing muscle tension or tightness? If so, where do you notice it? As you begin to connect to your body, it can help to focus on one sensation and follow it, tracking its subtle changes. As you track the different sensations one at a time, you will become more somatically connected, which will gradually broaden your somatic awareness of the various other sensations that are vibrating.

Tips: Because it can take some time to connect to your physical sensations, it can help to stimulate them with certain movements, thoughts, or objects. The following are a few tips to help you locate the sensations in your body.

- Place your right arm under your left armpit and place your left hand on your right shoulder, as if you were giving yourself a big hug. Now squeeze tightly, smile gently, and take a deep breath. After a moment, release your embrace, allowing your arms to fall to your sides. Pause, and notice what sensations you become aware of.

- Place your left hand on your belly and your right hand over your heart. If it feels natural, allow yourself to subtly rock side to side, as if rocking a baby. Take a deep breath and then bring your attention to your body. Do you notice any sensations? How is the energy in your body moving? What do you notice about your breath?

- Find two different objects and hold one in each hand. Bring your attention to the object in your right hand and notice its size, weight, and texture. Now bring your attention to the object in your left hand and notice its size, weight, and texture. Now compare the two objects. How do they feel different? How do they feel similar? Now set the objects down and return your attention to your hands. What impression did the objects leave? How are your hands reacting to the experience of holding the objects? What other sensations do you notice?

(Audio for this exercise is available at http://www.newharbinger.com/45243.)

Observe

To observe is to sit in awareness of your body sensations without judging them. It is to notice and accept what is happening in your body as it is happening, without pushing it away. Observing the energetic shifts in your body keeps you anchored in the here and now and awakens you to your felt-sense experience. So often we try to avoid or override our sensations because they are uncomfortable or because we think they are bad and we shouldn't be having them. Or sometimes we try to explain why we are having them so they make sense to us. For example, as you feel your sensations you may notice that you have an ache in your neck and then automatically think it's because you slept on it wrong. That may be the case. Or it may not. Either way, the purpose of observing is simply to notice that you are having the sensation of a neck ache, not to determine where it came from. To think about where it came from takes you out of the present moment and away from the potential of your sensations to offer insight into their deeper meaning.

If your impulse to think tries to hijack your efforts to observe, be kind to yourself. This is normal. We are neurobiologically hard-wired to make judgments, to create stories, and to wander down memory lane. Should this happen, lovingly remind yourself that you are not perfect, nor are you required to be. Mindful Somatic Awareness takes practice to cultivate; it doesn't happen overnight. Gently guide your attention back to your breath and your body sensations. With patience and self-compassion, your ability to observe your sensations will improve over time.

Pause and Observe

Return to the above "Pause and Sense" exercise. As you engage in the exercise and connect to your body, notice what sensations you become aware of. As the sensations emerge, observe them. What do you notice about them? Do they move? Do they intensify or soften? What are the characteristics of the sensations—do they have a color, texture, or size? Sometimes as you observe your sensations, you might get an image of how they may look, like Mary's description of the boating knot. Should an image come to mind, take note of it and see how your body responds to it. Also, observe the reactions you have to your sensations—do other sensations arise in response to them? You may find yourself getting frustrated and want to stop or force movement. You may also find yourself feeling more anxious in anticipation of what may come up. With each of these reactions, simply observe them without acting on them. Inevitably, they will give rise to other sensations. Should thoughts creep in, gently bring your attention back to your body and notice your body's reaction to your thoughts. What new sensations do you become aware of? Thoughts are energy, so your body will respond to the energetic pulse of your thoughts with its own energetic shifts.

(Audio for this exercise is available at http://www.newharbinger.com/45243.)

Articulate

To articulate your sensations means to describe them. It is to put into words the experience of the felt sense you observe. For example, as you bring your attention to your body, you might sense a lump in your throat. As you sit and observe the lump, you may begin to feel that it has certain characteristics, such as a rough texture, a green hue, or a shape like an almond. As you recall, Mary noted that the knot in her stomach looked "blue" and reminded her of a "boating knot." The sensations you experience can become more nuanced and specific the longer you sit in observance of them. You may also notice them changing and moving. Articulating the details of the sensations you observe helps distance you from them without disconnecting you from them. This keeps you from feeling overwhelmed by your sensations and organically calms a heightened fear response.

Sensations are raw and wordless when they emerge. They can also be intense and flood your body, which feels confusing and disorienting. When this happens, the sensations can take over, activating a fear response. Before you know it, you are lost in your sensations, no longer able to distinguish yourself from them—you become your sensations; you become your fear. Articulating your sensations slows things down so you can piece apart the sensations, differentiating them from one another, making them feel less intense and overwhelming. It also enables you to differentiate yourself from your sensations, so you are no longer identified with them. Rather, you are simply experiencing them. When you do this, it creates a sense of command over your sensations; it enables you to contain them so you can reflect on the thoughts, emotions, and behavioral impulses associated with them. This helps you understand your sensations and use the information they offer to ease your anxiety.

Pause and Articulate

Return to the "Pause and Sense" exercise. As the sensations emerge, observe them, and notice their variations and the subtle ways they shift and move in your body. As you observe your sensations, begin to articulate them, describing what they look and feel like to you. If you feel comfortable, try describing them out loud. For example, you might say, "I notice tingling in my calves; it feels like the static you see on TV." Or you might say, "I have tension in my head. It feels like I am wearing a helmet. I also notice that my shoulders feel heavy and strained. I have the impulse to take the helmet off my head." As you track your sensations and articulate the unique way they vibrate, ask your sensations: *If you could speak, what would you tell me?* As an answer comes to you, articulate it aloud. Articulating your sensations out loud acknowledges them. It makes them real in a way that is different and more powerful than when you do it silently in your mind. As you articulate your sensations, play with different adjectives and images. If you notice an impulse to move in a particular way, describe the impulse aloud and allow yourself to move. There is no right or wrong way to describe what you are sensing. If your effort to describe your experience resonates and feels right to you, then you are capturing the essence of your felt-sense experience. And the better you are able to articulate your felt-sense experience, the greater your awareness of it becomes.

(Audio for this exercise is available at http://www.newharbinger.com/45243.)

Reflect

To reflect is to sit in contemplation of your felt-sense experience. It is to explore with curiosity the messages embedded in your sensations so you can begin to cultivate a deeper understanding of your anxiety. As you begin to cultivate Mindful Somatic Awareness, learning about your felt-sense experience becomes an important part of understanding the origins of your fear and how it contributes to your anxiety.

Reflection might seem like it contradicts the purpose of Mindful Somatic Awareness because it requires thinking, which can take you out of the present moment. However, when you reflect while in a state of Mindful Somatic Awareness, you are engaging both the left and right hemispheres; you are integrating the insight gleaned from your felt-sense experience with logical thinking, giving you a deeper, more detailed understanding of your anxiety. This is essential for preventing or mitigating an anxiety response in the future. Reflecting during Mindful Somatic Awareness can yield undistorted information about what you were feeling and why you were feeling it. It can help you identify patterns of responses to certain sensations and environmental triggers. It also highlights the corresponding thought processes and belief systems that were activated with those triggers. This can tell you a lot about your anxiety, such as what provokes it and why.

Anxiety is often triggered outside our awareness. This is because the implicit memory at the root of anxiety is unconscious. Often, it isn't until you find yourself feeling the symptoms of anxiety that you realize you have been triggered. At that point you may be baffled as to why you are feeling this way. Or you may be able to identify what triggered your anxiety, but you are not certain as to why something is a trigger. Reflecting during Mindful Somatic Awareness enables you to connect to implicit memory that can help you understand your anxiety triggers and the cognitive processes and behavior responses associated with them. With this insight, you can also identify and begin to challenge the core beliefs you hold about the source of your anxiety.

I strongly recommend that you write your reflections in a journal when you can. Much like articulating your felt-sense observations aloud, writing down your reflections makes your process real in a way that is more powerful than when they exist solely in your mind. Journaling helps to clarify the thoughts, beliefs, and feelings as they come to you. And because the brain works in association, as you write down your reflections, they will reveal their linkage with other thoughts, beliefs, and emotions. With continued writing, your reflections will eventually weave together a meaningful context for your felt-sense experience. Further, because journaling with pen and paper engages both the body and the mind, it can slow your process and keep you present in the here and now.

Pause and Reflect

Once you have spent some time sensing, observing, and articulating your felt sense, begin to reflect on what you experienced. Start first by bringing your attention to your breath, inhaling through your nose and exhaling through your mouth. Then bring your attention to your feet, feeling the ground beneath them. Next shift your awareness to your seat and to your back. Feel yourself supported by the chair. Stay with your breath and the experience of physical support until you feel ready to open your eyes. Once you open your eyes, slowly look around the room to give your eyes a chance to adjust to the light and reorient to your surroundings. Sometimes opening your eyes after they have been closed for a while can be overstimulating. If you experience this, take as much time as you need to reacclimate. Then, with pen and paper, answer the following questions:

- What sensations did I experience during the exercise?

- What reactions or impulses did I have in response to my sensations?

- As I noticed my sensations, what were they telling me? What would they say if they could speak?

- What thoughts, emotions, or memories come to mind now as I consider my sensory experience?

- What might these thoughts, emotions, or memories reveal about the origins of my anxiety?

- What beliefs do I have about the thoughts, emotions, or memories I experienced?

- Did the experience of sensing my body make me feel anxious? Why?

- Did the experience of sensing my body make me feel relaxed? Why?

- What do I notice happening in my body right now as I reflect on my experience?

These questions are simply prompts to initiate your reflective process. Should you begin to write freely and break from the prompts, I encourage you to do so and follow your organic process. The more you are able to free-associate to the various thoughts, emotions, memories, and other cognitions that arise, the more you will connect to your implicit memory. Doing this will bring your unconscious emotional life into your conscious awareness, thereby deepening your understanding of yourself and, more specifically, your anxiety.

(Audio for this exercise is available at http://www.newharbinger.com/45243.)

To SOAR is to be fully aware in body and mind. The acronym is an easy-to-use, step-by-step guide to help cultivate Mindful Somatic Awareness so that you can become more successful at mitigating your anxiety and initiating mindful action. In this way, SOAR becomes the literal and metaphoric goal of anxiety relief—you want to SOAR through moments of fear and worry. The more you SOAR, the more natural it will feel and the more automatic it will become. You will find that when you are feeling overwhelmed and frustrated, or when you are experiencing a general anxiety that you cannot shake, SOAR-ing will help mute the ambient noise that frazzles you and reconnect you to your somatic core. From this place you can experience a natural softening of the anxious tension that inhibits your ability to respond authentically to the present moment. From this place you can also access your felt-sense knowing and your logical thinking so that you can begin to explore more deeply the origins of your anxiety and take steps to resolve the fear that resides there. The remainder of this book helps you do this. The chapters that follow highlight various sources of anxiety common to everyone and provide you with exercises that incorporate SOAR to help you know yourself more completely and grasp more fully the implicit origins of your anxiety.

CHAPTER 3

Reconnecting to Your Somatic Self

Your somatic self is your body self. And it is through your body self that your sensory experience resonates. Each unfolding moment strikes a sensory chord that vibrates throughout your entire body, giving rise to your felt sense of being alive. The sensations you feel carry with them information about your experience of the present moment—your sense of self, your sense of others, your sense of your surroundings. Further, sensations activate feelings, thoughts, and beliefs that inform your perceptions and behaviors. To illustrate this, take a moment to pause and close your eyes. Bring your attention to your breath until you feel grounded and more body-aware. Now visualize the smile of someone you love deeply, your best friend or favorite person, for example. As you do this, what do you notice in your body? How does it respond? What sensations are you aware of? Do you experience a sense of warmth, well-being, and reassurance that they are a part of your life? What thoughts or memories come to mind? What corresponding impulses do you experience? For example, do they bring a smile to your face? Do you feel the urge to hug them or give them a call?

The experience of a best friend is one whose meaning becomes known to you by how you feel in your body when you think of them or when you are around them. Intellectually, you understand that a best friend is a significant person who brings joy and meaning to your life. But when you think of *your* best friend, the value of that individual is made known to you by the unique way they make you feel; you know that they are deeply important to you because of the sensations that come to life in your somatic self. The information in these sensations not only tells you that you love this person, but also connects you to all the reasons why you love them. These sensations, like all others, are vital to your ability to navigate your life and relationships. They are integral to understanding your feelings, thoughts, and behavior patterns. And just as you can identify the thoughts and sensations associated with your best friend, so too you can learn the thoughts and sensations associated with your anxiety. As you foster your ability to connect with your sensations and allow them to flow without blocking their course, you can learn a great deal about your anxiety at a deeper, more meaningful level. You can then use this information to guide your efforts to heal the emotional pain and fear that keeps you from engaging in life with an open mind and heart.

Unfortunately, many of us have become inattentive to our body and are often unaware of feeling much at all. Even feelings of well-being can go unnoticed. When we do become aware of our body, it is often because it has become flooded with intense emotion, such as fear, powerlessness, anger, disappointment, or sadness—all very uncomfortable feelings that we then try to manage by distracting ourselves in order to disconnect from them. The result is that we are not very proficient in managing big feelings, nor are we familiar with the often subtle, nuanced way they vibrate. Consequently, the guidance these sensations offer to help navigate our lives remains unknown to us and our anxiety persists.

It is important to note that although many of us intentionally try to disconnect from our body to manage uncomfortable and over-whelming feelings, sometimes the disconnection happens automatically without conscious effort. The clinical term for this is *dissociation,* although it is often experienced as feeling foggy, numb, detached, or cut off. When this happens, highly distressing emotions, sensations, and physiological states are split off from conscious awareness with the intention of preserving functional integrity (Schwartz and Maiberger 2018; Ogden and Fisher 2015). Sometimes the experience of being dissociated is so complete that there is no awareness that you are cut off from your somatic self. Other times the disconnect is faintly perceptible, like a subtle knowing that something is *off* and that you are not feeling something you should be feeling (such as fear or concern). Instead, you feel numb, blank, or detached from your emotions and physical sensations.

It is easy to rationalize the experience of dissociation, believing that the disconnect means you are simply not having a reaction to whatever is going on. It takes time to learn the difference between feeling dissociated and feeling embodied and regulated. We will cultivate your ability to do this using the exercises throughout this book. In the meantime, it is simply important to know that dissociation is a phenomenon that happens involuntarily and that it is your body's way of protecting you and helping you survive emotional stress.

Whether it happens automatically or you initiate it through distraction, disconnecting from your body is not inherently bad. This might seem like a contradiction, but to unhook yourself from big feelings that disrupt your ability to think clearly, see objectively, and choose nonreactively can actually be helpful. Sometimes you come across moments in your life when the emotional stress is too high to manage. In these instances, you need to unfasten your right hemisphere from your left so you can preserve your psychological integrity while remaining physically present. It's like shifting into autopilot to manage the rush until the dust settles and you can return to your life in a more embodied way. Problems arise when, after the storm has passed, you do not reengage your body and reflect on the impact the situation or circumstance had on you. The moment may have passed, but the experience remains in your body, recorded in your implicit memory.

Ideally, the goal is to regulate your nervous system so as to decrease your overall anxiety. You also want to build somatic integrity and resiliency, so you can improve your ability to tolerate heightened fear and other intense emotional responses. This is what Mindful Somatic Awareness helps you achieve. However, whether you remain embodied or detached during times of fear or stress, reflecting on your experience in Mindful Somatic Awareness is imperative for anxiety relief. Creating time specifically to return to your body enables you to connect to the implicit information that got wired in when you were overwhelmed so that you can understand the emotional impact of the experience and integrate it into your present awareness. Additionally, it facilitates nervous system regulation by helping you settle any emotional charge and physical unease that remains in your body. When your body is regulated, your thoughts become clearer and your feelings become more manageable. When you overlook this process, your nervous system may remain activated, keeping you anxious and acutely sensitive to environmental triggers. You also miss a valuable opportunity for reflection that may yield greater insight into your fear response. Neglecting to pause and sit in Mindful Somatic Awareness is very common, as my client Thomas illustrates perfectly.

Thomas came to see me for help managing his anxiety. His anxiety symptoms began after he experienced a panic attack following an incident at work. Thomas is a top executive at a large-scale corporation. Among his many roles as an executive is the unfortunate task of terminating employees. For years Thomas flew all over the country delivering shattering news to dozens of individuals. According to Thomas, he could do this without difficulty because "it wasn't personal." However, one day, following his latest firing, he returned to his hotel room, where he began to experience trembling in his body, shortness of breath, and dizziness. Thomas was having his first ever panic attack. Though he was able to settle his panic, a low-grade anxiety persisted thereafter.

As we explored the possible origins of his panic attack and subsequent anxiety, I got to know more about Thomas. I came to experience him as a very kind man with a gentle spirit. And though there were clearly other parts of his personality that allowed him to excel in the corporate world, underlying his commanding stature, self-assuredness, and obvious business acumen was a deeply feeling individual who had a notable capacity for empathy and compassion. This made it difficult for me to accept his assertion that he was not bothered by the multitude of terminations he had delivered over the years. Someone with a heart like Thomas's could not fire people so easily without it leaving an emotional mark. I shared this with him and asked if he would open his mind to the possibility that stored in his body was the cumulative effect of the emotional impact of having fired all those individuals: that a part of him feared the possible devastation it could have on their lives, but that he did not allow himself to consider this or feel it because he was powerless to do anything about it. With apprehension, Thomas agreed to play with this possibility.

To begin, I had Thomas bring his attention to his breath and then expand his awareness to the rest of his body, allowing him to connect with the various sensations it was vibrating. I then asked him to return to the moment at work before his panic attack, the moment when he let an employee know that he was being terminated. With his eyes closed, he described the room in which the firing took place. As Thomas recreated the visual in his mind, he began to experience trembling in his body. He immediately opened his eyes and explained why he was likely trembling. "I drank an extra cup of coffee this morning because I didn't sleep well last night," he said. "That could be it," I replied. "But since we have the time, let's just play with the possibility that it is related to what you were describing. If you'd like, maybe try it with your eyes open— that might feel more comfortable for you." Cautiously, Thomas agreed. Eyes open, he returned to the scene and immediately began to tremble. Again, Thomas quickly engaged in conversation, taking himself out of his sensations (right hemisphere) and into thinking (left hemisphere). When I reflected back to him what appeared to be a tendency to disengage his body when he began to experience uncomfortable sensations, he acknowledged it, stating, "I don't like the way it feels. I can't control it."

The Origins of Somatic Disconnect

Like many of us, Thomas didn't like not being able to control the uncomfortable sensations in his body. He didn't know how to make sense of them because they contradicted what he thought he felt. Thomas thought he was okay with firing the employees who worked for his company. His body, however, felt very differently about the matter. That is to say, it actually pained his heart. So, to manage the dissonance, he cut off his feelings and lived in his thoughts, a place where everything made sense and there was no emotional distress that threatened the veracity of his logic and reason.

Thomas's efforts to cope with uncomfortable feelings reflect what we all do to varying degrees. That is, we all take ourselves out of our body in order to help manage feelings we don't understand or that seem overwhelming and disempowering. For example, distracting yourself from your anxiety by filling your day with a laundry list of things to do helps you disconnect from your body. Though there can be some relief in feeling productive, this does not fully assuage your anxiety because your body still holds the fear. Another common coping strategy is reframing your perspective to see everything positively. This is an intellectual exercise that denies the experience of the body. And though a positive shift in perspective may reflect a more accurate assessment of reality and foster hope, your body still holds the fear, and so an undercurrent of anxiety will continue to flow.

Now, these coping strategies are not inherently bad. I would even encourage them at times as they can be helpful in mitigating anxiety and making you feel more empowered. But in the end, if you are not returning to your body in Mindful Somatic Awareness to understand and integrate the implicit imprint of your experiences, you remain in somatic disconnect. Consequently, the relief you experience from distracting yourself from your anxiety will be short-lived—the body will always insist that its voice be heard.

The Imprint of Your Formative Years

Although we are neurobiologically designed to disconnect from our bodies to help us remain psychologically intact when we are emotionally overwhelmed, we are not designed to live in a state of disconnect all the time. In fact, nature has evolved us specifically to use the sensory cues from our body to alert us to environmental signals of safety, danger, and threat (Porges 2011). Our sensations are a vital component of our emotional, physical, and psychological survival.

So how does it come to be that we can move so far away from our somatic selves and all the vital information that dwells there?

Using the somatic lens to answer this question, we focus on the implicit memory recorded in our body during our formative years. Doing this helps us understand our tendency to neglect the emotional life of the body and disconnect ourselves from uncomfortable feelings. The unconscious somatic memory that was wired in during your early development can reveal how you learned to cope with feelings and to understand emotional experiences. And though implicit memory continues to actively archive experiences throughout your life, it is the implicit memory that was wired in during your early life that can reveal a great deal of information about the coping mechanisms that activate during times of stress and how this contributes to your present fear and anxiety.

Neurobiologically, children experience and make sense of their surroundings in predominantly sensory and emotional ways. Their reasoning abilities are nascent. When children experience a lot of intense emotions, this can flood their little nervous systems. You can liken this to pouring a gallon of liquid into a cup—the cup is far too small to hold the contents of a gallon of liquid. In the same way, the child's nervous system is too small to hold the emotional charge of big feelings without an adult to help contain and explain them. If a child doesn't have an adult to make sense of things and comfort their emotional self, or if the adults in their life are overwhelmed and dysregulated, then the child has to find a way to manage these big feelings on their own. Disconnecting or distracting is a perfect solution to help regulate the flood of feelings. These early experiences are implicitly wired in as default ways of regulating emotions, and they can show up again in adulthood during times of fear and stress. This is why, as an adult, you may have a reasoned perspective that is grounded in insight gleaned from lived experience and still find yourself irrationally fearful that something bad will happen. Stored in the nooks and crannies of your unconscious memory system are old ways of seeing similar situations as well as an old instruction manual for how to cope with the way those situations made you feel. And if disconnecting or distracting were also ways the adults in your life coped, then odds are that your young mind-body took note of this and recorded it in that very same instruction manual.

As children, we turn to the important adults in our lives to help us navigate the often confusing and frightening terrain of emotional experiences. In the upcoming chapters, we will explore how your coping strategies were informed by the primary caregivers in your life and how this contributes to your anxiety. We will also look at how your primary coping system emerged from significant events in your life. This will yield greater insight into your fear response. For now, simply be mindful of your emotional reactions to your environment. Be curious about them and ask yourself: *I wonder why I responded that way? Where would that come from? What would happen if I responded differently?*

Let's return to Thomas to look more closely at the origins of his somatic disconnect and how he was able to detach from the distress he would often feel when he fired employees. Thomas grew up in a family that was not emotionally expressive or affectionate. There was no hugging or other loving physical contact. There was not much conversation, either. Dinners were eaten largely in silence. His parents inquired very little about his experiences at school, his friends, or the musings of his inner world. Rather, they focused their attention on his achievements, which never seemed to be good enough. This often left Thomas feeling hurt, frustrated, and powerless. Despite this, Thomas said he felt loved by his parents, appreciating the material provisions they faithfully provided and recognizing that they parented him the best they could. Through Mindful Somatic Awareness, however, Thomas came to realize that despite his parents' love, their lack of affection deeply impacted him.

One day in session, while practicing Mindful Somatic Awareness, Thomas spontaneously remembered an incident as a young boy when he was at the house of a friend. His friend's father was rolling on the ground, playfully wrestling with his friend's younger siblings. As Thomas looked on, he remembered thinking, *That's how it's supposed to be. That's what's missing.* It was a memory that initiated a flood of emotion and a felt-sense awareness of the degree to which the cold emotional climate of his childhood affected him and how it created in him a chronic longing for the warmth of physical affection and emotional connection. To cope with this longing as well as with the hurt and frustration he felt when his efforts to please his parents failed, Thomas distracted himself. He used sports and academic endeavors as a way to occupy his mind and to disconnect from emotional pain. However, at the time he did not know that that was what he was doing; it was an unconscious adaptation to the emotional conditions of his home—adaptations that he carried into adulthood.

As our work progressed, Thomas connected to his innate nature as a deeply feeling individual, sensitive to both his own feelings as well as those of others. He came to see how important emotional needs were not met when he was a child, and also that he was not taught how to understand and manage his own emotional experiences. Somatic disconnect was the only way his young mind-body could get him through the pain and confusion. He also saw how this same coping strategy enabled him to fire employees without concern despite knowing it could devastate their lives—if he didn't feel it, it wouldn't bother him. Without his feelings gnawing on his heart, he could rationalize his actions by telling himself it wasn't personal. But despite his best efforts to disconnect from his body, the experience of each termination was implicitly wired in and his somatic self eventually demanded that he tend to it. Through Mindful Somatic Awareness, Thomas was able to decrease his anxiety and develop coping skills that did not require him to silence the voice of his body—coping skills that instead fostered sustained connection to his body and, therefore, to his heart.

Reconnecting to Your Somatic Self

The following is a series of exercises designed to help reconnect you to your somatic self and facilitate your ability to SOAR. When you first engage in these exercises, you may experience discomfort. This is because the experience of your sensations is unfamiliar and unknown to you, which can feel unsettling. Plus, there was a reason why you disconnected from them in the first place—you didn't like the way they felt, as they were very unpleasant and uncomfortable. But your sensations will not destroy you. In fact, the information they carry has the profound ability to help you heal. Further, the beauty of coming home to your body through Mindful Somatic Awareness is that you will also reconnect to all the wonderful sensations you missed out on in trying to avoid the bad ones. It may take time to feel comfortable with these exercises, but be patient: if you practice them regularly, you will benefit from their gifts.

Breath

Breathwork is an essential component of anxiety relief. When your body is fearful and anxious, your breathing becomes shallow and rapid. Often there is tightness in your chest, making it difficult to inhale deeply. This is because when you are anxious, your sympathetic nervous system is activated and your body is preparing to mobilize a survival response. Increased heart rate and rapid breathing help the body do this. But for the anxious person, constricted breathing can become a fixed breath pattern, causing you to get stuck in a feedback loop where your anxiety causes shallow breathing and your shallow breathing triggers your anxiety. (When the SNS is activated, even when one isn't anxious, it can trigger anxiety. This is because the physiological experience of arousal is the same as the physiological experience of anxiety. So rapid, shallow breathing can actually cause or trigger anxiety. It can also reinforce it.) The way out of this cycle is to engage your parasympathetic nervous system through focused breathwork. This will help regulate your breathing and aid in bringing your body back into a state of calmness.

Shallow breathing can also be a source of somatic disconnect. When airflow to the body is constricted, so too is energy flow, which means that our range of feeling is restricted. This is purposeful, since it is advantageous for the body to feel less when it is preparing to defend itself against threat or danger. But when shallow breathing becomes a fixed pattern, it can also become a fixed way of coping with uncomfortable sensations and their corresponding emotions and thought processes. As you begin the following breathing exercise, you may experience anxiety as you connect to the very sensations you have been trying to avoid. Should this be the case, pause and use the resourcing and orienting exercises that follow to bring you back into the present moment and help regulate your nervous system.

Find Your Breath

Using a carpeted floor, a mat, or a towel, find a quiet place where you can comfortably lie on the floor. Now, bend your knees and press your lower back into the floor. Keep your feet flat on the floor about a foot or more apart. Place one hand over your heart for compassion and one hand on your belly so you can feel it rise and fall with each breath. Now gently breathe in through your nose and out through your mouth, allowing your rib cage and belly to fully expand with each inhalation and to fall with each exhalation. Do not force a deep breath. If one comes naturally then allow it, but forcing a deep breath can be anxiety inducing. Be sure to exhale completely, as it is the exhale that supports relaxation. As you engage in the exercise, your breath will naturally deepen and find a rhythmic flow. After several minutes, when it feels right to you, SOAR: sense, observe, articulate, and reflect.

You can also practice this breathing exercise while sitting in a chair. The purpose of lying on the floor is to take the stress of gravity off the body and provide support for the back. This facilitates a greater opening of the chest and the belly to release the tension that is often held there.

(Audio for this exercise is available at http://www.newharbinger.com/45243.)

Resourcing

Resourcing is the practice of generating positive sensations of safety, strength, comfort, and optimism and then focusing on those sensations to calm your body (Payne, Levine, and Crane-Godreau 2015). By consciously shifting your attention away from sensations of anxiety toward sensations of well-being, resourcing helps teach your nervous system to regulate stress. It also fosters resiliency, enabling you to better tolerate the feeling of being overwhelmed and to recover from adversity. Examples of resourcing are a fond memory or a favorite person, pet, or place. It can also be something more active, like dancing, listening to music, or engaging your inherent talents and passions. A resource is anything that helps to calm feelings of unease and moves your body back into a natural state of health and harmony. The following is a resourcing exercise I have found to be very helpful with my clients. If it works for you, great. If not, find your own resource and use it during times of anxiety or any uncomfortable sensation you need help regulating. You can also resource when you are in a state of calmness, as practicing this exercise will strengthen its efficacy during times of stress.

Best Friend

Find a quiet place where you will not be distracted. Once you feel settled, close your eyes and bring your attention to your breath. Take three deep breaths, inhaling through your nose and exhaling through your mouth. Now think of your best friend, or a person you love and adore. Describe what they look like—their hair, clothes, and smile. Imagine their eyes and what you see when you look into them. Imagine the sound of their voice and their laughter. Think of their mannerisms and any unique aspects of how they move their hands, walk, or speak. As you do this, memories or playful jokes you share may come to mind. Entertain these recollections and invite your body to respond to them in whatever way arises. For example, if you instinctively smile, allow that. If you instinctively laugh, allow that. Now, as you sit in the imagination of your best friend, SOAR.

(Audio for this exercise is available at http://www.newharbinger.com/45243.)

Grounding

Grounding is attuning to the feeling of contact between your feet and the ground. It closes the gap between you and the earth, inviting a sense of security and safety. With anxiety, we often feel "up in the air" or "ungrounded." This is because anxiety brings us upward into our head and away from our body and its contact with the earth. Grounding reanchors you in your physical body and reconnects you to all the sensibilities that reside there—those innate and often unconscious sensibilities that help you navigate life and living. Bringing your attention to your physical body and its deep connection to the earth *grounds* you in the present moment. It also facilitates feelings of strength, stability, and resilience where we feel we can "hold our ground" and "stand on our own two feet." In this way, grounding can be very effective in bringing immediate relief from the distress and powerlessness of anxiety. Grounding can be as simple as noticing the contact between your feet and the floor when you are sitting in a chair at work or standing in line at the grocery store. Simply bringing your attention to the sensations in your feet and the feel of their connection with the ground can restore a sense of calm in your body.

Find Your Ground

Find a quiet place where you will not be disturbed. Stand with your feet about a foot apart. Bend slowly forward toward the ground as far as you can go. If you can, touch the floor with your fingers. Keep your knees slightly bent. Be sure not to lean forward putting weight onto your hands. Keep all your body weight in your feet. Let your head drop and dangle, allowing its weight to stretch your spine. Be sure to breathe—in through your nose and out through your mouth. Hold this position for as long as feels comfortable.

Now slowly pull yourself upright, one vertebra at a time. Once you are standing upright, take three slow breaths. Now, with your knees slightly bent, make a fist with each hand and place them in the small of your back, knuckles facing inward. Bring your shoulder blades together and stick out your chest, your belly, and your buttocks—you'll feel a bit like a duck. Breathe in deeply and exhale completely three times, allowing your rib cage and belly to fully expand and releasing any tension you hold there. This position can feel mildly stressful. But you will find that when you release the stretch, you also release the stress held in your muscles. Hold the pose for as long as feels comfortable and then relax. Now, find a chair where you can sit, attune to your body, and SOAR.

(Audio for this exercise is available at http://www.newharbinger.com/45243.)

Orienting

Orienting is the act of directing your attention to the space around you and noticing all its various attributes. All animals instinctively orient to their external environment to assess for safety, danger, or threat, and we are no exception. However, we often become so busy in our everyday life that we rarely stop to notice the space around us. Additionally, if we are anxious, we tend to orient toward aspects of our environment that remind us of our fears, with the unconscious intention of finding evidence to support our belief that we should be afraid. Or, if we happen to notice aspects of our space that indicate safety, we don't always trust those indicators. When we fail to consciously notice our environment, or if we orient only toward aspects of our environment that support our fears while disregarding those that signal safety, we perpetuate and often intensify our anxiety. In doing so, we ignore our instinct to know the space around us and use the information it offers to regulate our nervous system. Orienting to your surroundings and simply noticing, without judgment, the specific attributes of your environment naturally modulates the nervous system and brings you back into the here and now.

Know Your Space

This is an exercise you can do pretty much anywhere, any time. Begin by bringing your attention to your breath and then to your body, taking note of the various sensations you are experiencing. When you are more body-aware, shift your attention to the space around you. Really take in all the various attributes of the environment—sight, sound, smell, touch. Slowly turn your head to the right and then to the left, taking in a panoramic view of your space. What do you see? Who do you see? What do you hear? What attributes of your environment are of particular interest to you or catch your attention? What colors are you aware of? Name these things aloud and describe them. What happens in your body as you name and describe each person or thing? Pay attention to how your body responds to what you are noticing. As you reflect, consider why you might notice some aspects of your space more than others. What do they remind you of? What thoughts do they generate? As you do this, intermittently pause and SOAR.

Often when our anxiety is particularly acute, expanding our field of vision to take in the entirety of our environment can be overwhelming. If you find your anxiety increasing as you begin to orient, focus your attention on one thing in your space that you have a positive association with. Name the thing aloud and describe it. Once you have done this and it feels safe to shift your focus, orient toward something else in your space with which you have a positive association. Do this slowly, piece by piece, until it feels safe to widen your visual scope and notice more completely the space around you.

(Audio for this exercise is available at http://www.newharbinger.com/45243.)

Breathing, resourcing, grounding, and orienting are not only exercises that can help you reconnect to your body, they are also powerful methods to bring your nervous system back into a state of calmness once your anxiety has been activated. So, should your anxiety get triggered as you engage in the remaining exercises in this book, return to one of the aforementioned exercises to calm your activation before continuing the exercise.

Anxiety feels terribly uncomfortable in your body. The impulse you have to distract or disconnect from sensations of fear not only is natural, it's understandable. However, when you restore your relationship with your somatic self, you facilitate your body's intrinsic ability to regulate feelings of fear and alleviate your anxiety. You also come into conscious awareness of how your body communicates feelings of fear, which demystifies the often confusing sensations that vibrate when you're anxious. As we move into the next chapter, we will take a closer look at the different ways your body lets you know it is afraid. We will explore the various aspects of your fear response so you know exactly what is happening in your mind-body and why. You will also acquire more tools to help you tolerate a heightened fear response, so you can more quickly and efficiently regulate your nervous system and mitigate your anxiety.

CHAPTER 4

Anxiety and the Fear Response

In the preceding chapters, you learned that encoded in your implicit memory system is the origin of your anxiety. Additionally, you learned that this very system also provides access to the wisdom your body holds to resolve the fear that perpetuates your anxiety. We discussed how your somatic self is always vibrating with sensation and how these sensory vibrations carry with them an abundance of intuitive information about you and your surroundings. When these vibrations are deciphered by reasoned thinking, the information they offer can help you reduce your anxiety, support mindful action, and guide your efforts to heal your unresolved fears at a deeper level. We have also taken steps to reconnect you to your somatic self so as to enhance your awareness of these sensory vibrations. But the question remains, *How do I interpret somatic information? How do I know what my sensations are communicating to me?*

In this chapter you will learn to interpret somatic information as it relates to your anxiety. More specifically, you will learn to break apart and understand your fear response. Your fear response is the physiological, behavioral, and cognitive reaction you have to real or perceived threat or danger; it is the instinctive response you have to stimuli, a response that triggers defensive behaviors intended to protect your psychological and physiological self. To understand your fear response is to understand your anxiety. This is because your anxiety is a chronically activated fear response. When you are anxious, your body is afraid and preparing to protect itself against threat; it is primed and ready to preemptively mobilize survival behaviors to avert what feels like an inevitable crisis. In the following pages you will become acquainted with the unique way your body communicates signals of fear, as well as the behaviors and thought processes associated with them.

Understanding your fear response is essential to anxiety relief. To begin, the ability to identify what triggers your fear response facilitates right and left hemisphere integration, helping to regulate your nervous system and enable mindful action. As we discussed, your fear response originates in the lower brain (the brain stem) and the midbrain (he limbic region, both of which are regulated predominantly by the right hemisphere. However, *identifying* the fear trigger is a left hemisphere process, one that also helps you understand what is happening in your body and why. Once the trigger has been named and your corresponding reaction is understood, you can then begin to think about and work with the situation or circumstance to determine mindful action. However, you can take the process further. When you know the unique way your fear response expresses itself and have determined the trigger, you can use Mindful Somatic Awareness to explore the implicit memory (or memories) that caused you to perceive the stimulus as frightening or overwhelming. Understanding the deeper, unconscious dynamics of your anxiety reveals its historical origins. When you know why a stimulus acts as a trigger for your anxiety, you can begin to understand and heal the unresolved fears it is linked to. With this information, you can also begin to challenge your perceptions. In this way you can see and experience the stimulus as nonthreatening, so that it no longer activates your fear.

The Basics of a Fear Response

An effective fear response is dependent on the mind-body's ability to detect and interpret sensory information from the external environment around you and the internal environment within you. So as you seek to understand your fear response, what you are seeking to understand is the unique way your sensory system detects and perceives information from the environment and how it integrates this information into behavioral, cognitive, and emotional responses intended to protect you from threat or danger (Porges 1993). Later in this chapter I will introduce three sensory feedback systems that help facilitate this process. For now, however, it is important to give you a basic understanding of the physiological, behavioral, and cognitive symptoms common to a fear response, so you can learn the unique way your mind-body responds to threat or danger.

Physiological Symptoms of a Fear Response

A fear response is instinctive and initiates a cascade of physiological processes that prepare the body to mobilize protective action, such as fight, flight, or freeze. These bodily processes include the release of stress hormones that facilitate swift and efficient use of energy to ensure the success of your protective efforts. Some of the changes experienced include accelerated heart rate and breathing, dilated pupils, and a decrease in digestive activity. Blood flow is pulled away from the extremities and toward the larger interior muscles and organs. This explains the cold and clammy hands and feet common to anxiety. Additionally, your brain becomes hypervigilant and acutely responsive to environmental stimuli. The list of physiological changes that prepare the body for defense is long and varied, but each body is different and, therefore, each body has its own unique presentation of symptoms. Your work is to increase your awareness of *your* physiological experience of fear, because this will increase your understanding of your anxiety.

My Body and My Fear Response

The following is a list of physiological symptoms of a fear response common to anxiety. Read through the list and identify the symptoms you experience when you feel anxious. Write them down somewhere.

List of Physiological Symptoms

Shortness of breath

Holding your breath

Accelerated heart rate

Tightness in chest

Sweaty palms

Cold and clammy hands and feet

Muscle tension

Trembling or feeling shaky

Nausea

Diarrhea

Upset stomach

Dizziness

Pit or butterflies in stomach

Forgetfulness

Hot flashes

Chills

Numbness

Tingling sensations

Acute startle response

Sleep disturbance

Fatigue or exhaustion

Grogginess

Hypervigilance

Difficulty concentrating

(This list is not exhaustive. If you are aware of physiological symptoms you consistently experience when you are anxious, but they are not listed here, write them down and consider them a part of your own unique fear response.)

The physiological symptoms of fear and anxiety are very uncomfortable and can make you feel like you don't have control over your body. This can exacerbate anxiety. The simple task of identifying the physiological changes related to anxiety is an important step in regulating it. Knowing what is happening in your body and naming the symptoms aloud regulates the fear response—these are the sense, observe, and articulate components of SOAR.

You can also take this process further. Remember that when you experience a fear response, your body is actually doing exactly what it is designed to do when it believes danger is imminent—to protect you. The problem is that you are perceiving threat or danger where there isn't any. So, once you have named the physiological symptoms aloud, find the compassionate voice in your heart, close your eyes, focus on your breath, and tell yourself the following: *"Right now, I fear that something bad is going to happen, because once upon a* time something bad did happen, and for reasons I am still trying to understand, I think the bad thing will happen again. This is why my body is feeling fear: it is trying to protect me. And I thank you, wonderful, strong body, for responding in this way to ensure my survival. And I also kindly tell you, beautiful body, that what I feared then is not in the present and there is no longer a need to be afraid."

Before moving on, it is important to note that the above symptoms reflect the physiological changes initiated by the sympathetic nervous system (SNS) and are associated with fight or flight. But remember, the fear response also includes *freeze*. As noted in chapter 1, freeze happens when the parasympathetic nervous system (PNS) shuts down SNS activation in situations where fight or flight is ineffective or not possible. During the PNS shutdown, certain physiological, behavioral, or cognitive faculties are no longer available. For example, your mind goes blank and you can't think or speak. Or you suddenly feel paralyzed and can't move. Additionally, you may feel fogginess, grogginess, and fatigue, as well as a heaviness in your body, or the need to lie down and take a nap. Other symptoms include excessive yawning, belching, and other gastrointestinal activity. For example, my client Angela yawns incessantly whenever she processes her anxiety around setting boundaries with her family. She also loses strength in her body, making it difficult for her to sit upright. Inevitably, she collapses and curls up into a ball in the chair. These are all symptoms indicating acute PNS activation. Keep this in mind as you begin the process of learning about your own fear response and what activates it, because you may have some anxiety symptoms that reflect high PNS arousal.

Behavioral Symptoms of a Fear Response

When your anxiety has been activated, there is an instinct to quickly do something to manage the uncomfortable feelings or prevent the feared thing from happening. These reactive behaviors are part of a fear response and are commonly known as "fight, flight, or freeze." However, in the human mind-body, these behaviors can creatively morph into sophisticated protective and defensive responses. For example, among the most common fear response behaviors is avoidance. Avoiding situations or people that activate your anxiety and make you feel a loss of control is a very common way to prevent encounters with highly stressful or threatening situations. My client Nick does not engage in any activity in which he will not excel because he does not like to be confronted with his own limitations, nor can he tolerate not being able to control others' perceptions of his limitations. These situations activate his feelings of inadequacy, his expectations that others will perceive him negatively, and his fear that these negative perceptions are irreparably damaging and have the power to adversely alter the trajectory of his future. It is not surprising that he also struggles with perfectionism, which also helps him manage these fears. Until our work together, avoidance and perfectionism were among the ways Nick controlled his anxiety around feeling inadequate and insecure. He is not alone. We all have our own repertoire of behavioral responses that help us manage our anxiety.

The following is a short exercise to acquaint you with your fear response behaviors so that, when they arise, you know your anxiety has been activated and you can begin to challenge yourself to try a different approach.

My Behavior and My Fear Response

The following is a list of fear response behaviors common to anxiety. Read through the list and identify those behaviors you engage in when you feel anxious. Also, add any behaviors you engage in that are not listed. The next time you find yourself doing one of the listed behaviors, pause for a moment. Describe the behavior aloud. Then ask yourself: *What am I afraid will happen if I do this differently?* Then SOAR. Attune to the sensations that vibrate when you consider changing your behavior. Observe, without judgment, the way those sensations vibrate in your body. Articulate aloud what you are sensing, and then reflect on why it is you are engaging in those behaviors. Ask yourself why you are afraid and why you think this particular behavior will help. If it is not feasible for you to pause in that moment, take a moment later in the day. Sit in a quiet room, close your eyes, and imagine yourself engaging in one of the fear response behaviors. Now ask yourself the same questions and SOAR.

List of Behavioral Symptoms

Avoidance

Overcompensating or overfunctioning

Obsessive thinking

Overchecking

Escaping

Refusing to go out and away from home

Restlessness or fidgetiness

Perfectionism

Being judgmental and critical of others

Jumping to conclusions

Fixed and rigid routines

Limiting or reducing daily activities

Limiting or reducing social engagements

Being irritable or short tempered

Addictive behaviors

Self-medicating

Keep in mind that engaging in fear response behaviors is not inherently harmful. In fact, these protective responses are necessary. They are vital for your psychological and physiological survival. They become unhealthy and problematic when they become fixed and unyielding, when they inhibit goal-setting, creativity, authentic self-expression, intimacy, and overall feelings of joy and pleasure.

Cognitive Symptoms of a Fear Response

The cognitive processes of a fear response refer to the thought patterns and core beliefs associated with the unresolved fear-based experiences that activate when your anxiety has been triggered. These fear-based thoughts and beliefs adversely imbue the lens through which you see yourself and the world around you; they can negatively influence your assessment of people, situations, and circumstances as well as your perceptions of how future events will unfold. Additionally, they tend to be inflexible and unrelenting, they inhibit necessary risk-taking to achieve goals, and they coerce certain decisions and behaviors that keep you from living authentically. What makes them even more problematic is that they are often unconscious and automatic, influencing the way you see and do things without your even knowing it. This is why cultivating a deeper awareness of the cognitive processes related to your anxiety is imperative to your healing process.

In the next chapter I will expand more on the origins and impact of fear-based thoughts and beliefs. However, it is important to introduce them now, so you can begin to consider how they are entwined in your fear response and perpetuate your anxiety.

Over-Coupling and the Fear Response

When exploring your fear response and the corresponding physiological, behavioral, and cognitive processes, it is important to understand the phenomenon of *over-coupling* (Levine 2005). Over-coupling occurs when different fragments (sensory stimuli, physiological reactions, behaviors, thoughts, and emotions) of an overwhelming or frightening experience become unconsciously linked or coupled together (Levine, Selvam, and Parker 2003). These over-coupled fragments bind together so tightly that they are instantly associated with one another when reexperienced, even when there is no threat or danger. Here is a simple example of over-coupling: John is sitting in his car at a stoplight, patiently waiting for the light to turn green. Suddenly he is hit from behind by another car. Now, whenever John approaches a red light he feels terrified that he will get rear-ended again. In this example, the stoplight and getting rear-ended have become over-coupled and trigger a fear response in John. Over-coupling also occurs in relational dynamics. For example, when Katie was a child she struggled to learn math. Her mother would often grow impatient and frustrated with her while helping Katie with her math homework. Further, when Katie's test scores did not meet her mother's expectations, her mother would simply look at her with quiet disapproval and walk away. For Katie, failure or mistakes became over-coupled with disapproval and the withdrawal of love, along with the thoughts, emotions, and sensations she experienced in those moments with her mother. Now, in her present relationship with her boyfriend, when Katie believes she has let him down or has disappointed him, she experiences acute anxiety that he will stop loving her and leave her.

Over-coupling is a dynamic phenomenon involving many aspects of the mind-body. However, we will focus our attention predominantly on the unconscious cognitive components of the over-coupling process. When over-coupling occurs, an unconscious narrative emerges that attempts to make sense of and give meaning to the frightening or overwhelming experience. This narrative is then used (often unconsciously) as a guidebook for navigating similar situations in the future in order to prevent the same thing from happening again. The template of the narrative goes something like: *If this happens, then that will happen* (Levine, Selvam, and Parker 2003). For example: *If I tell him I can't attend the party, then he will be disappointed in me*. Or: *If I make a mistake, then she will think I am incompetent*. Or: *If I don't do her this favor, then she will think she is not important to me*. Each of these narratives has physiological, emotional, cognitive, and behavioral components—components that, when coupled together, create the blueprint of your fear response. Though some over-coupled aspects of an overwhelming or frightening experience may be clear and distinct, many over-coupled fragments are unconscious, existing largely in your implicit memory. This is because over-coupling is a process that occurs predominantly in the brain stem and limbic region of the brain. Mindful Somatic Awareness can be used to reveal the over-coupled fragments of unresolved fear experiences at that deeper level.

In the next chapter I will elaborate on the concept of over-coupling and its connection to negative thoughts and core beliefs. For now, however, it is useful to acquaint yourself with the general over-coupling narratives you have, so as to understand the cognitive processes of your fear response.

If This, Then That

This exercise is intended to begin the process of exploring the negative thought patterns and core beliefs connected to over-coupled fragments of unresolved fears in your implicit memory. Begin by completing the phrases below. Write as many examples of each as you can think of. Then set your list aside. You will be using your list later to help explore the deeper dynamics of your anxiety.

If this happens _____, then _____.

If I do this _____, then _____.

If I say this _____, then _____.

When All the Symptoms Come Together

To demonstrate the phenomenon of over-coupling as well as the various ways a fear response may present itself, I will share with you Janine's story. Janine reached out to me for help managing her anxiety, which she described as a "chronic buzz" in her body. She also experienced times when her anxiety would spike and she would feel "panicky." When this happened, she noticed that her lungs felt tight and it was hard to breathe. Additionally, she felt trembling in her limbs, tension in her muscles, and heart palpitations. Also noteworthy was a sense of urgency that overwhelmed her, as if she was "racing against a clock" and she had to hurry up and do something before time ran out. As we began to explore her anxiety, I asked Janine if she knew what triggered the panicky feeling. She noted that it always happened at work when she thought she had made a mistake. She said she would frantically obsess about how she could fix the mistake while at the same time fearing that it was irreparable. A similar thing would also happen in her relationships when she thought she had done something wrong. In these instances, Janine would fixate on repairing the damage done from her wrongdoing, often going above and beyond to overcompensate for her mistake. But regardless of her efforts to mend the situation, she always felt a sense of dread that her misstep was unforgivable.

One day I asked Janine if she could tell me what, in her mind, constituted a mistake. After a short pause, she said, "When I disappoint someone or let them down." "How do you know when you let someone down?" I inquired. "I don't know," she replied, "I can just tell." Intrigued, I pressed on. "You mean, they don't get upset with you and tell you that you disappointed them?" "No, not that I can think of," she answered. "But they don't have to. I can see it in their face."

Janine had no real evidence to support her belief that she had made a mistake or let someone down. Nevertheless, she was adamant that she had. This strongly suggests that an important piece of Janine's anxiety was concealed in her unconscious somatic memory. It was evident that her anxiety was linked to a chronic fear of making mistakes and that this fear was coupled with a fear of disappointing others. But the proof that supported her belief that she had made a mistake and let someone down was based primarily on her perception of the other person. That is, how she read their face. This told me that implicit information was being used to interpret and understand the situation. So the question now became: *What nonverbal sensory information is linked with the experience of disappointing others? And what is so frightening about disappointing others? Why would this create such dread?* When I posed this question, Janine's response intrigued me. "I don't really know, but it feels like it would be very bad."

Going Deeper: Exteroception, Proprioception, and Interoception

Like Janine, many of you are familiar with your anxiety triggers. However, you may not always know why they are triggers in the first place. Or you may have a good understanding of why something triggers your fear, but there are times you nonetheless find yourself baffled as to why you feel anxious, because, as far as you can tell, none of those triggers are identifiable in the current situation. This is because it is not just your conscious awareness that is assessing and interpreting the present moment, but also your unconscious awareness—your implicit memory system.

What follows is an introduction to three important sensory feedback systems in the nervous system that, when attuned to, can help you access implicit memory and reveal more information about your anxiety triggers, especially those triggers that are more indistinct. The information gleaned from attuning to these systems can take you deeper into the folds of your anxious mind-body. In doing so, the dynamic interplay of the physiological, behavioral, and cognitive components that generate your fear response is illuminated. Further, it exposes the various fragments that over-coupled during the original fear-based experience. Identifying these fragments enhances your ability to detect the most subtle of anxiety triggers, so you are no longer bewildered by your reactions.

The three sensory feedback systems are: exteroception, proprioception, and interoception. They are response systems in the nervous system that communicate with the mind-body about the space around you, within you, and where the two meet. It can help to think of them as a current of information that flows on a continuum, with exteroception at one end of the continuum, interoception at the other end, and proprioception in the middle. The flow of information along this continuum is constant, and the interchange of information among the three feedback systems is dynamic—with each one informing the others at all times. When you can quiet your mind-body and connect your somatic self to the movement of this energy-information flow, it generates a powerful felt-sense experience that can illuminate important implicit aspects of your fear response.

Exteroception

Exteroception refers to the sensory experience of your external environment and asks the question, "What is happening in the space around me?" Exteroceptive awareness includes what you see, hear, smell, taste, and touch. When exploring the hidden dynamics of your anxiety, we must consider implicitly recorded exteroceptive details of the original frightening or overwhelming experience—the unconscious recording of what your mind-body saw, heard, felt, smelled, and even tasted during the emotionally distressing event or circumstance.

Proprioception

Proprioception is the ability to sense the movement of your physical body. It also facilitates perceptual awareness of the position and orientation of your body in relation to your surroundings. Proprioception acts like a navigation system that guides your movement within the space around you simply by sensing where things are. This is why you can walk around without paying attention and not bump into things, Proprioception also enables you to move your limbs accurately without looking at them, as when you touch your finger to your nose with your eyes closed or move your foot from the gas pedal to the brake. Additionally, proprioceptive awareness gives you a sense of balance, and it lets you know when you are sitting upright or leaning to the side. And if you are leaning to the side, proprioception gives you a sense of the effort you need to exert to prop yourself back up. As you can see, proprioceptive awareness is a felt-sense experience. Through Mindful Somatic Awareness, it can yield an abundance of implicit data recorded during the original overwhelming or frightening experience at the core of your anxiety.

Interoception

Interoception is the heart of Mindful Somatic Awareness because it is, simply stated, the ability to sense the internal states and processes of your body. Interoceptive awareness attunes to the unique way sensations vibrate throughout your somatic self. This can include the sensory awareness of thirst, hunger, and sleepiness as well as less distinct sensations such as temperature, tension, and itch. Sensory feedback provided by interoception communicates to you how you are perceiving and experiencing the external world, which in turn influences your internal world, including your thoughts, emotions, and behavior. Like proprioceptive awareness, interoception gives rise to a felt sense of self in the present moment and can reveal implicit memory related to your anxiety.

The following is a Mindful Somatic Awareness exercise that integrates exteroceptive, proprioceptive, and interoceptive awareness with SOAR to help you create real-life situational or circumstantial contexts in which your anxiety gets triggered. It takes you deeper into the folds of your anxious mind-body and exposes the over-coupled fragments of the original frightening or overwhelming experience. Further, it facilitates an increased capacity to interpret the somatic information related to your anxiety while also illuminating the dynamic interplay of the physiological, behavioral, cognitive, and emotional components that cause your chronic fear and worry.

Diving Deep

Retrieve the over-coupling narratives you listed in the previous exercise ("If This, Then That"). While seated in a quiet room, review the list and choose a narrative that resonates with you the most in this moment. Before you continue, remember that should your fear activate beyond what feels comfortable, return to the breathing, resourcing, grounding, or orienting exercises to help bring you back into a state of regulation. Once your fear has subsided and you feel ready, resume the exercise. If your body struggles to calm itself, put the exercise aside for another time when your body feels more able to regulate the charge of the feelings and sensations that get activated.

To begin, close your eyes and bring your attention to your breath until you feel more body-aware. Now say the narrative aloud. As you say the narrative aloud, notice what happens in your body. Next, imagine a scenario, from either your childhood or adulthood, where the narrative activates and you experience anxiety—a situation you fear or one where you believe you must think or behave in a particular way, because if you don't, you will experience negative consequences.

Once you have such a scenario in mind, invoke exteroceptive awareness and create the sensory experience of the external environment. What do you see? Who do you see? What do you hear? What are you aware of touching? What might be touching you? What do you taste? Create a detailed picture and describe your exteroceptive awareness aloud.

Once you have created a dynamic, external context, begin to imagine yourself in the space you created and invoke proprioceptive awareness. Where are you in relation to other people and objects in the space? How are you moving in the space? What does it feel like to move? Do you feel free to move or do you feel inhibited? Do your best to create a felt-sense awareness of your somatic self in the space you have created and speak this awareness aloud.

Now bring your attention to your interoceptive awareness. What sensations activate in your body as you imagine the space around you and yourself within that space? Notice each region of your body and what you are sensing there—your shoulders, your belly, your calves, and your feet. Do specific details of the space trigger a physiological reaction? If so, what details are activating and why? Notice your breath as you observe your interoceptive experience.

As you bring your exteroceptive, proprioceptive, and interoceptive experience together, broaden your awareness to other aspects of your process. Notice what thoughts come to mind as you visualize the scenario and your physiological reaction to it. What emotions do you notice? What is your instinctive behavioral response? What do you feel compelled to do? Now, imagine doing it. What do you sense when you imagine doing it? If you're not able to honor your impulse to respond in a particular way, why not? What is your response to that?

Sit with this scenario for a bit. Allow yourself to move freely along the continuum of exteroceptive, proprioceptive, and interoceptive feedback. Throughout the exercises, intermittently pause to SOAR so you can integrate your mind and body processes. Sense your physiological reactions, observe them without judgment, and articulate them aloud. Then reflect—allow yourself to consider why it is you are having these reactions. Ask yourself: *What do I believe would happen if I reacted differently? Why do I believe that?* As you ask yourself these questions, notice what happens in your body.

If you can stay with this process and surrender to its organic unfolding without coercing or editing your response, you will uncover important information about your anxiety—information that previously remained unknown to you. Additionally, you will create an opportunity to discharge the emotional energy bound up with the unresolved fears in your nervous system. This cathartic release of emotional energy is a powerful healer that can lift a heavy heart and shift perspective, bringing you relief from your anxiety.

To help you further understand the purpose and efficacy of this exercise, I will return to Janine. Janine's insight into her anxiety was good. She knew that among her triggers was a fear of making a mistake. She was also cognizant of what happened in her body when she experienced fear. Additionally, she was aware of a cognitive process that told her if she made a mistake, she would disappoint others. And she was aware of the overwhelming sense of urgency that prompted a behavioral response to quickly rectify the mistake she believed she had made. But what remained unknown were the nonverbal signals from her environment that told her mind-body she had disappointed others. What also remained a mystery was the reason why disappointing others was so frightening. What was this "bad thing" that would happen if she let someone down?

One day in therapy, after using Mindful Somatic Awareness to connect to her body, I asked Janine to imagine a scenario where her fear of making a mistake was activated. She immediately associated to an incident that happened over the weekend when she visited her mother. Her mother had asked Janine to stop and pick up some snacks and sandwiches. Janine was reluctant because her mother is notoriously hard to please, and even though she asked her mother specifically what she wanted, Janine nonetheless feared getting the wrong thing. Sure enough, when she reached her mother's house, her mother took one look at the chips Janine had purchased and said scornfully, "Why did you get these chips? They're full of salt." Then she opened the sandwich bag and sneered, "Why did you get me a whole sandwich? I can't eat all this." According to Janine, her mother then appeared irritated, flitting about the kitchen with terse, sharp moves, pursed lips, and short huffs of breath. Needless to say, Janine's anxiety spiked. To no avail she attempted to calm her mother by letting her know she would return to the store to buy low-sodium chips and that, if she cut her sandwich in half, she could save the rest for another time.

I asked Janine if there was a reasonable voice in her head that told her that her mother's chronic dissatisfaction was her mother's issue and had nothing to do with Janine. She said, "Absolutely! She's the most discontented woman ever; nothing pleases her. And yet, she still has the power to make me feel bad and I don't know why." At this point I asked Janine if she felt comfortable exploring this a little deeper. She eagerly agreed. I had Janine close her eyes and visualize herself standing in the kitchen with her mother. I then guided her awareness to her exteroceptive experience of the space. Though she described the kitchen in detail, she paid most attention to the look on her mother's face—her brow, her lips, her eyes. I then asked Janine to describe her proprioceptive experience. "It feels like my mother is standing right in my face, even though she is actually several feet in front of me, behind the kitchen counter." With this, I inquired about her interoceptive experience. "I feel frozen," she replied. "There is a dark tightness in the pit of my stomach. My shoulders feel heavy and want to curl in, and my knees feel weak and want to buckle."

Without prompting, Janine associated to a childhood memory. One day when Janine was a young girl, her mother asked her to do the dishes. As Janine was drying the plates, she accidentally dropped one and broke it. Hearing the commotion, her mother ran into the kitchen, stopping short of the broken glass on the floor. As Janine told the story, she began to weep. Through her tears, she recalled that the look on her mother's face back then was the same look she saw this weekend, a look of utter disappointment. "I can see her furrowed brow and her pursed lips, her eyes squinting at me with shame and disapproval." As Janine continued, she noted how *bad* her mother's look made her feel. It made her feel incorrigible, rejected, and unlovable. And, as children often do, Janine believed the feelings she experienced were true: that she was, in fact, unlovable.

The development of a child is such that their sense of self is a felt one; it is sensory and emotional. So when children *feel* bad, they often think they *are* bad (Wilkinson 2010). Janine was no exception. For Janine, the *bad* thing that would happen if she disappointed someone by making a mistake was to reexperience the devastating feelings of rejection, unlovableness, and shame. This fear originated in her relationship with her mother when, as a child, Janine was admonished with shame for making mistakes. Through her body language, her vocal tone, and the look in her eyes, Janine's mother communicated her disapproval and disappointment. The sensory fragments experienced during these moments all coupled tightly together and were wired into Janine's implicit memory. Now, when triggered in present time, they gave rise to the same felt sense they generated then: rejection, shame, and unlovableness. And the "chronic buzz" Janine experienced in her body was connected to a chronic anticipation of reexperiencing these awful feelings; the chronic anticipation of making a mistake, the stress she experienced in her efforts to repair the mistake, and the despair she felt when she considered the futility of her efforts. To cope with her anxiety, she had always sought to be perfect or flawless, to avoid making mistakes altogether. However, striving for perfection merely added to her stress and anxiety, because being perfect is simply not possible.

Janine's example illustrates the powerful influence of unconscious and unresolved emotional pain on our physiological, emotional, cognitive, and behavioral reactions. It demonstrates the subtle but potent impact of over-coupling, how sensory fragments of fear-based experiences that link together and live in our implicit memory can so quickly and sweepingly determine our perceptions, and how automatically and resolutely they interpret feelings as reality. Most strikingly, Janine's example draws our attention to how emotionally charged experiences in early childhood shape us, and how those same experiences come to life in our adult minds to help us understand and make sense of ourselves and the world around us.

Now, with greater understanding of your fear response and the implicit memory that activates it, you have increased awareness of your somatic experience of anxiety. But what about your cognitive experience of anxiety? That is, how does the anxiety you feel in your body impact the reasoned thinking of your mind? In the following chapter we will move up the spine and into your mind to answer this question. We will revisit the cognitive components of your fear response and trace their origins to your somatic self so as to illuminate the dynamic interplay between your feeling body and your thinking mind.

CHAPTER 5

Anxiety, Negative Thoughts, and Core Beliefs

In this chapter we are going to focus on negative thoughts and core beliefs. This time, however, we will take a closer look at how they contribute to and perpetuate your anxiety. We will peer through the somatic lens to see how your negative thoughts and core beliefs were formed, how they influence your felt sense of self and others, and how they shape your mindset and sway your choices and behavior. Additionally, we will foster insight into the way your negative thought patterns express themselves in your emotional responses and how this hinders authentic self-expression and inhibits the ability to be fully present in the here and now. Finally, you will learn to use Mindful Somatic Awareness to uncover, challenge, and change the unconscious thoughts and core beliefs that perpetuate your anxiety so you can shift your mindset and engage in your life with confidence, hope, and optimism.

The somatic lens shows us that thinking is a mind-body phenomenon. That is, thought patterns and core beliefs do not emerge exclusively from left hemisphere processes. Rather, our right hemisphere, with its strong connection to the brain stem and limbic region, evaluates the emotional significance of our experiences and attaches meaning to them while our left hemisphere enables us to think about those experiences to facilitate understanding of all their various aspects. Thinking, then, is an integrative process combining intuitive knowing that comes from the body and logical reasoning that comes from the mind. However, when we were first born and in our early developmental years, we did not have an optimally functioning left hemisphere. In fact, left hemisphere functioning significantly trails right hemisphere functioning during that time in our life. Thus, the core beliefs and the thought processes that emerge from early experiences are primarily the work of the emotion-driven right hemisphere and reflect the logic of a child. Because of this, deeply held core beliefs are often untrue. Further, because they are generated primarily from right hemisphere processes, they are tucked away in our implicit memory and remain unknown to us. This becomes problematic when these core beliefs cause anxiety and inhibit authentic, purpose-driven living. My client Stephen demonstrates this perfectly.

When my work with Stephen first began, he had little awareness of the negative beliefs and thought processes that were keeping him stuck in a job he disliked and in a relationship that was unfulfilling. He just knew he was afraid of making changes that would improve his circumstances. In my conversations with Stephen it was immediately evident that his thought processes were swayed by negative core beliefs about himself and others. Though I did not yet know what they were, I could see that those core beliefs influenced his thinking in such a way that he talked himself out of choices that could change his circumstances, ultimately sabotaging his efforts to improve his life. Curious to unveil the hidden cognitive processes that kept him stuck and the childhood experiences from which they emerged, I inquired about his early history.

One of four children, Stephen was the youngest by seven years. The notable time gap that separated Stephen from his siblings, who were all born within a couple of years of one another, created for Stephen the experience of feeling like an outsider. His entreaties to play were frequently turned down by his siblings, who were absorbed in the happenings of their own teenage world and indifferent to the interests of their little brother. Desperate to foster a connection with them, Stephen recalled a time when, during arts and crafts at school, he made for his oldest brother a clay sculpture of a football. His brother was a football fanatic and Stephen's young mind thought this gesture would endear him to his brother and prompt him to invite Stephen to play catch in the yard and maybe even hang out in his bedroom. But Stephen's fantasy was crushed when his brother said nary a word about the sculpture, let alone about the longing-filled thoughtfulness with which Stephen made it. Making matters worse for Stephen, his mother and father both worked long hours and were rarely home. When they were around, they were busy running errands and catching up on household chores. Throughout his young life, Stephen longed for someone to play with, to engage and connect with, but that need was never met with any consistency or reliability. This left him feeling lonely and unimportant, as if he wasn't a priority to the people he loved.

As my work with Stephen progressed, he revealed himself to be a deeply caring, sensitive, and contemplative man with a strong tendency to put his own needs aside to ensure that others were happy. As a manager, he would often stay after hours at work to help his employees, even if it meant he would miss important appointments. As a boyfriend, he would assume his girlfriend's responsibilities, such as running her errands and washing her car. And in therapy, Stephen would often take care of me, making sure that the issues he was working through weren't making me uncomfortable.

One day Stephen entered therapy feeling particularly upset about an incident that had happened with his girlfriend a few days earlier. It was her birthday and Stephen, always thinking of thoughtful ways to demonstrate his affection for her, wanted to surprise her with her favorite meal and then take her to a movie she'd been wanting to see. However, things didn't go as planned. With the kitchen table all set, adorned with flowers and balloons, and the aroma of homemade lasagna and garlic bread wafting through their home, his girlfriend walked through the door, took off her coat, and stood at the head of the table. "What's all this?" she asked. "It's for you," Stephen answered, beaming with delight. "I made your favorite meal: lasagna and garlic bread. Later I thought we could go see a movie." "That's sweet, thank you," she replied. "But I'm tired and not really hungry. I think I'm going to go lie down and watch some TV." And off she went.

After Stephen had relayed this story to me, I asked him how he felt about his girlfriend's response to his thoughtful gesture. He said it bothered him, but that he chose not to say anything. When I asked why he kept his feelings to himself, he said that he feared that talking about it might upset her and he didn't want to do that on her birthday. I validated his reasoning, but also asked a question intended to challenge it. "Your care for others' feelings is a wonderful quality, Stephen, but what about *your* feelings? Who cares for them?" "I never really thought about my feelings," he said. "I've noticed that," I replied, "and I can't help but wonder if that has something to do with why you feel anxious and stuck in your life."

Stephen is a common example of how we often react or adapt to situations or circumstances in unconscious ways. Until I pointed it out, Stephen had had no idea he was dismissing his own feelings and how doing so might be connected to the fear that inhibited his efforts to effect change in his life. Further, because he was unaware of this, he was also unaware of the thought patterns and belief system that rationalized his choices and perpetuated the behavior patterns that kept him stuck in his fear. Our goal then was to uncover the unconscious thought processes and their emotional and physical correlates, in order to relieve his anxiety and dislodge him from these behavior patterns. Once again, we turn to early childhood to facilitate this understanding.

The Origins of Negative Thoughts and Core Beliefs

When we use the somatic lens to explore the origins of our belief systems and the thought patterns that emerge from them, we see that they originate in infancy and continue to develop and change over the course of our lives (Ogden and Fisher 2015). However, as noted above, in our early developmental years, our meaning-making processes are under the powerful influence of our felt-sense experiences, of both the past and present. This is because in children the right hemisphere is still at the helm of the meaning-making process, with the left hemisphere sitting in the passenger seat. With the right hemisphere in charge, the subjective experience of a child is emotionally driven and personalized. That is, experiences and the emotional meaning a child attaches to them are often seen by the child as being about the child or because of the child, even if they are not. Further, children often interpret their emotional experiences as absolute truth, especially when those emotions are big and overwhelming or the situations in which they arise are consistent and repeated. Over time, these truths are wired in as core beliefs, which generate thought patterns, which in turn influence perceptions and behaviors. We then carry these cognitive processes into adulthood and (often unconsciously) use them to help us navigate our lives. So if your early life carries the weight of significant and repeated frightening, overwhelming, confusing, disappointing, or hurtful experiences, then many of your present-day core beliefs and thought patterns likely emerged from those experiences and ended up being significant contributors to your anxiety.

As you may recall from the previous chapter, Janine's early *felt* experiences of disapproval and rejection from her mother made her *feel* unlovable. This feeling was interpreted by her child mind as *truth* and was wired into her somatic self as a core belief—*I am unlovable*—a belief her body held about who she was and how she could expect to be treated. This then influenced her perceptions of others and her behavior patterns in relationships. Janine's story demonstrates how cognitive processes organize around emotional and physiological correlates that inform our sense of self, others, and the world around us. It illustrates how our child's thoughts and beliefs develop through *felt-sense* experiences and become *felt processes* recorded in our somatic memory that inform our cognitive processes in adulthood. This is why it is so important to consider your early developmental years when trying to understand the thought patterns and belief systems associated with your anxiety. To do this, it is helpful to revisit the concept of over-coupling, as it is a simple way to understand how your cognitive processes interface with your physiological, behavioral, and emotional responses.

Unconscious Coupling and Conscious Uncoupling

When it comes to the thought patterns and core beliefs associated with your anxiety, the ultimate goal is to deactivate them. Further, we want to wire in new cognitive processes that enable open-mindedness to the countless possible ways of experiencing reality as it unfolds in each moment. But because thinking is a mind-body phenomenon, we know that if we use only our logic and reason to do this, we won't be able to make lasting change in our cognitive patterns; we will inevitably lapse into old ways of thinking. In order to change our negative thoughts and core beliefs, we need to understand their connection to our body and target them there, too. This will create lasting change in the way your mind-body sees, thinks about, and experiences reality. Let's return to the phenomenon of over-coupling to help us with this.

To recap, over-coupling occurs when different fragments (such as sensory stimuli, physiological reactions, behaviors, thoughts, and emotions) of an overwhelming or frightening experience bind tightly together and become unconsciously associated with one another. During this process, you construct a narrative that attempts to make sense of and give meaning to what happened. Contained within this narrative are certain thought patterns and core beliefs about yourself, others, and the world. This narrative is then archived in your implicit memory and referenced (much like a guidebook) in the future to help you navigate what your mind-body perceives as similar situations. These narratives carry the thought patterns and core beliefs associated with your fear and anxiety.

As you can see, over-coupling demonstrates how the cognitive processes associated with your anxiety live in your mind *and* body. Our goal, then, is to use Mindful Somatic Awareness to identify the implicit cognitive processes connected to your anxiety and their dynamic interplay with your physiology. We also want to uncouple or loosen the over-coupled fragments of your fear response. When the over-coupled fragments of your fear response begin to break apart, it creates space for new information to flow in and inform your felt-sense experience and, therefore, your perception. Uncoupling also has the effect of increasing the time you have to respond in moments when your anxiety has been triggered. That is, it reduces your reactivity, and when you are less reactive, you have more time to identify what you are feeling *and* thinking and employ mindful action.

Remember, the over-coupled fragments are bound together so tightly with fear that, when triggered, they initiate a reactive response that happens so quickly you don't always realize it. This reactivity inhibits adequate left hemisphere participation in your experience, so your behavioral response is not well integrated with reasoned thinking. Without a logical assessment of the situation or circumstance, mindful action is not possible. Furthermore, when your adaptive response is reactive and driven by your right hemisphere, you remain stuck in the fear-based narrative related to your over-coupling.

Keep in mind, your reactive response stems largely from over-coupling, which carries with it your fear-based narrative. When operating under the influence of your fear-based narrative, your perception of reality will reflect that. That is, your perception will reflect the expectation that bad things happen or *will* happen. This is because your fear-based narrative unconsciously holds the expectation that *what has been is what will be,* thereby influencing how you see and interpret the circumstances and events of your life. The expectation that the past will be recreated in the present or in the future creates a negative feedback loop that reinforces your anxious thought patterns and perceptions. It also reinforces the original over-coupling, keeping your mind-body stuck in a fear-based narrative that perpetuates your anxiety and inhibits new ways of experiencing reality.

The fear-based narratives, and the cognitive processes they carry, can be rigid and unyielding. Further, they dictate choices that inhibit authentic living and the expansion of your true self. The fear-based narratives tell you not to be vulnerable, not to take risks, and not to make mistakes. And so you don't. They tell you that others are not safe and cannot be trusted. And so you pull inward and close down your heart. They tell you that, no matter how hard you try, your efforts will not be rewarded. And so you do not try, or you only try half-heartedly. They tell you that your light does not shine as brightly as others. And so you dim the radiant light that shines within you, or extinguish it altogether. Fear-based narratives are so powerful that even if you take a risk *and* you get the best possible outcome, your mind will invalidate it. Echoing the sentiments of your narrative, your mind will tell you it was a fluke, an accident, and not to get your hopes up because it won't happen again.

However, when you uncouple your fear response and break apart the fragments that keep your mind-body constricted, you create an opening for new information to come through at a deeper level and change the way you think *and* feel about yourself and your experience. With this comes a change in your perceptions and an opportunity to rewrite your narrative. Uncoupling gives you the freedom to change your story to reflect a more life-affirming experience. It gives you the opportunity to change your thoughts and beliefs to reflect a consciousness that welcomes uncertainty because it has faith in your strength and resiliency. Further, uncoupling gives you the gift of time—time to integrate this new way of thinking into a generative perspective willing and able to see the countless possibilities that abound in each moment. When you uncouple, you no longer see the world through the lens of *what was*. Rather, you see the world through the lens of *what can be*.

The following is an exercise to increase awareness of your fear-based narrative and the thought patterns and core beliefs associated with it. It also uses Mindful Somatic Awareness to facilitate uncoupling and demonstrates how the expectations embedded in your fear-based narrative influence your perceptions and behaviors. In doing so, it creates an opportunity for you to rewrite your narrative and give new meaning to the original fear-based experience. With this new narrative come new thought processes and core beliefs that trust in the infinite potential that dwells within you.

As you begin to explore your thought patterns and core beliefs, it is important to keep in mind that they were created with the mind-body of the little you—the child you once were, whose subjective experience was emotionally driven and whose logic was simple and innocent; the little you who did not have an adult to help you understand your feelings and teach you that the bad things you felt were not your fault. Keep in mind, too, that the core beliefs that emerged from your fear-based experiences were intended to protect you, even if now they cause distress. Also, if the core beliefs you uncover seem so illogical or irrational that your instinct is to dismiss them, then this is likely an indication that you are on the right track. Again, it was your child mind-body that informed them, so they will naturally conflict with your adult reasoning. Lastly, you may experience guilt, shame, or other uncomfortable feelings as you engage in this exercise. This is very common when working through fear and anxiety. Please have compassion for yourself and remember that your core beliefs do not reflect some flaw within you. Rather, they reflect the mindset of a scared and confused child who was doing their very best to adapt to an uncertain, stressful, and overwhelming reality.

Negative Core Beliefs

Close your eyes, take a few deep breaths, and bring your attention to your body. When you feel more body-aware, open your eyes. Now review the following list of negative core beliefs and write on a separate piece of paper those core beliefs that resonate with you. Be sure to write them down the following way: *I believe I am…* For example: *I believe I am not good enough.* If you have a core belief not listed here, write it down.

I am worthless.

Failing is unacceptable.

I am a failure.

I am not good enough.

I am undeserving of love.

It is dangerous to care.

Love is too risky.

Love will go away.

People will leave.

I don't deserve success or happiness.

I am not likable.

I am not lovable.

People will not like me as I am.

People will betray me.

I will be rejected.

I am not smart.

I have to be perfect.

Intimacy and closeness are dangerous.

It's not safe to express my feelings.

Success will make me happy.

Life is burdensome.

I have to serve others' needs.

I must do what others want me to do.

I am destined to struggle.

Being single is scary.

Being dependent is scary.

Everyone is smarter than I am.

I will lose someone if I express my feelings.

Now, in a column next to your negative core beliefs, write down its opposite positive belief. For example, if one of your core beliefs is "I believe I am undeserving of love," write next to it: "I believe I am deserving of love."

Next, in a quiet place, settle into a chair with your feet flat on the ground. Close your eyes and bring your attention to your breath. Once you are more body-aware, open your eyes and state the first negative core belief on your list, for example, "I believe I am unworthy of love." Now, close your eyes and SOAR—sense, observe, articulate, and reflect. Notice how your body responds to the belief. What sensations do you notice?

Now, say aloud the opposite, positive belief. Close your eyes and SOAR. Again, how does your body respond. Does it reject the new belief? If so, how do you know? Does it accept the new belief? If so, how do you know? Pay attention to how your body responds to your existing core belief and the introduction of the new one. Note any resistance to the new core beliefs that you experience. Also note any openness to receiving the new core belief and what somatic response this generates in you.

Now return to the "If This, Then That" list of narratives from the previous chapter. Using that list, match each narrative with the core beliefs you marked from above. This will help you see how your narratives reflect thought patterns that are organized around your core beliefs. Each narrative may have multiple associated core beliefs. For example: "If I assert my needs, then I will be dismissed. I will be dismissed because I am not deserving of love."

Next, as you did above, in a column next to your thought pattern and core belief, write the opposite positive thought pattern and core belief. For example: "If I assert my needs, then I will be heard and responded to. I will be responded to because I am deserving of love."

After you have paired each narrative with a core belief and have written down its opposite, choose one narrative and core belief from your list that most resonates with you at this time. As you did above, say the negative narrative and core belief aloud and SOAR. How does your body respond to this belief and thought pattern? Track your reactions and consider the same questions you did in the above exercise.

Next, repeat the same thing with the opposite, positive core belief and thought pattern. Now SOAR. Notice how your body responds to the introduction of a new way of thinking about yourself and the world around you. Notice, too, the thoughts your somatic experience generates.

Let's return to Stephen to uncover how his young mind-body made sense of his childhood experience and how that meaning-making process morphed into core beliefs and thought patterns that kept him stuck in a pattern of living rooted in fear.

Stephen was upset and anxious after his girlfriend's lukewarm response to the surprise dinner he had made for her birthday. Yet he chose to keep his feelings to himself because he didn't want to upset her. Or at least that is what he told himself. I reminded Stephen of his earlier remark when he noted that he does not consider his own feelings. "I don't," he said. "What's the point?" "Let's try and answer that question by *actually considering your feelings* and see if that can help us understand your anxiety."

I asked Stephen to close his eyes, bring his attention to his somatic self, and track his sensations until he felt more body-aware. I then asked him to repeat what he had said a moment ago: "There is no point in considering my feelings." After he repeated the statement, I asked him to describe what he felt in his body. "I feel tightness, like my muscles are pulling in." As Stephen spoke, I noticed he crossed his arms tightly against his stomach. Then he said, "Now, my brow is getting heavy and my face feels like it wants to scowl." As I looked at Stephen, he definitely appeared angry, much the way children look angry when they pout. Even so, he didn't seem to be aware of his emotional experience, only his physical one. That is, there seemed to be a disconnect between his mind and body. So I asked Stephen to exaggerate his furrowed brow and scowl and to tighten his crossed arms.

As Stephen dramatized his body language, something clicked. He slowly released his grip, looked me square in the face, and said, "Oh my goodness, I'm angry. I never realized I was so upset. I can't believe she didn't acknowledge the time and effort I put into making her birthday special." I sat quietly and watched Stephen's mind-body animate as he connected to the sense of self-worth that entitled him to the experience of having his feelings considered. Noticing this, I asked Stephen to restate the opposite of his belief. "I am important, and my feelings deserve to be considered." As he did, I asked him to describe what he felt in his body. "Well, I feel a bit looser and lighter, which feels great. Though there is still some tightness in my muscles. It feels scary to relax them and accept this new belief. I can feel some anxiety about being let down again, even though I don't want to."

Stephen's resistance, though mild, was to be expected. He was not yet able to fully take in this new way of thinking because it was unfamiliar and couldn't yet be trusted; his mind-body was still wired to expect disappointment. But, importantly, there was a crack in his over-coupling, which created space for new information to flow in. Further, it created the flexibility needed to consider old information in a new way. This small but powerful slack in the over-coupling associated with his fear-based narrative created the opportunity for lasting and meaningful change in the way Stephen thought *and* felt about himself, others, and the world around him.

Over time, through Mindful Somatic Awareness, Stephen connected to the feelings of loneliness and rejection he had experienced as a child—feelings that remained deep within him even as an adult. He was able to see how his young mind had made sense of the repeated experience of being ignored by concluding that he was unimportant—a conclusion that had solidified into a core belief. Gradually this core belief influenced his thought patterns and produced a narrative about who he was and what he could expect from the world. For example, among Stephen's narratives was: *If I reach out, I get ignored. I get ignored because I am unimportant. Because I am unimportant, my needs don't matter and I do not get to have what I want.* Though this narrative is a cognitive process, it was ultimately anchored in the unresolved fear held in his somatic self—the fear of being ignored and reexperiencing profound feelings of disappointment, loneliness, sadness, and shame. This narrative was operating unconsciously in Stephen's mind-body and inhibited movement toward the things he wanted in his life. Further, this fear silenced his voice and the expression of his needs in his relationship. This is why Stephen did not communicate to his girlfriend the hurt and anger he felt when she barely acknowledged his birthday present—he feared the dismissal he had experienced as a child. He thought it better to not say anything and to adapt to the situation, because trying to change it would be futile and only make him feel worse.

When Stephen connected to his anger, what he really connected to was a survival response—the innate and sacred life-force energy within him specifically designed to protect and preserve his physiological, psychological, and emotional self. This was a turning point for Stephen in healing his anxiety, because in connecting to his anger, he no longer felt powerless; he was no longer at the mercy of his environment. Rather, he could use the energy from his anger to draw boundaries, to communicate to others how he felt, and to mobilize himself to create the change he so badly wanted in his life. Stephen finally felt a healthy entitlement to the voice of the child within him that, so long ago, wanted to say to his family, "Stop ignoring me! You're hurting my feelings. I'm scared and lonely." And he connected to the voice that wanted to say to his girlfriend, "I feel hurt by your response to my thoughtfulness, and it is not okay with me."

As the over-coupled fragments of Stephen's fear response loosened and he began to challenge old ways of thinking, feeling, and seeing, the expectation that he would reexperience rejection slowly dissolved. Further, as he connected to his inner strength and resiliency, he realized that even if he was dismissed or invalidated, he could tolerate it. That is, it would not destroy him *and* he could do something about it. Over time, the core beliefs that reinforced his expectations that the past would always repeat itself became deactivated. He was then able to rewrite his personal narrative and wire in new, life-affirming core beliefs that supported his voice and his healthy entitlement to ask for what he wanted and create the life he envisioned for himself.

The following two exercises will help you identify your negative cognitive processes and how they are linked with physical and emotional correlates, so that you can heal the old emotional wounds at the core of your anxiety.

That Was Then...This Is Now

Return to the list of negative core beliefs from the previous exercise. Now, connect each belief to a childhood memory. Once you have made this connection, SOAR—sense, observe, articulate, and reflect. Consider how those beliefs were helpful to you then. Think about how making sense of things in that way helped you adapt to overwhelming, confusing, or frightening circumstances.

Now, identify a recent adult memory or present-day situation or circumstance in which these core beliefs got activated. Once you have something in mind, SOAR. Consider how helpful and adaptive these core beliefs are now. Evaluate their efficacy.

Now, state the positive opposite of the core belief you identified. After you have stated this aloud, SOAR. Think about the situation from this new perspective. Is it more helpful? How does your body respond? Do you experience resistance to seeing things this way? Why might this be?

Compaooion for tho Child Within

Review your list of negative core beliefs and link them with childhood experiences or circumstances in which those negative core beliefs were formed. Now close your eyes and imagine yourself as a child in one of the experiences on your list. Imagine yourself feeling confused, scared, disappointed, angry, or hurt. As you imagine yourself as a child, also imagine the kind, compassionate, loving adult within you sitting with your child-self. Imagine your adult-self helping your child-self understand what is happening. Imagine your adult-self reassuring your child-self that everything is going to be okay and that nothing is your fault. Speak aloud to the child within you as you would any child—with love, compassion, understanding, and a desire to soothe their fears so that they feel safe and secure. As you do this, SOAR.

(Audio for this exercise is available at http://www.newharbinger.com/45243.)

With greater insight into the way the thought patterns and belief systems related to your anxiety emerge from the dynamic interplay between your mind and body, we are now ready to shift focus and explore how this influences your external perceptions. While it is vital to know and understand the world within you, ultimately, life requires that you engage the world around you. The following chapter uses the somatic lens to explore the way your anxiety affects your perceptions—the way you organize, interpret, and make sense of your surroundings. You will also learn to challenge those perceptions that perpetuate your fear and anxiety, so you can begin to see the world with new eyes and discover the infinite potential in each moment.

CHAPTER 6

Anxiety and Perception

On our journey so far, we have peered through the somatic lens to gain a deeper understanding of your anxiety and how to heal the unresolved fears that constrict your innate impulse to live freely and authentically. From the outside looking in, we have come to see the infinite and eternal intelligence contained in every cell of your body and how, when you pause in Mindful Somatic Awareness and feel the waves of sensations vibrating throughout your body, you are really pausing to *feel* the vibration of that intelligence—to feel the intuitive knowing of your somatic self. Throughout the previous chapters we have followed the guidance inherent in your somatic intelligence and have come to know various aspects of your anxiety—the diverse ways you disconnect from your body to protect yourself from uncomfortable emotions and situations; the unique dynamics of your fear response and the stimuli that trigger it; and the unconscious thoughts and beliefs that keep your mind-body mired in a personal narrative that invalidates or distrusts the infinite potential that dwells within you. Now, however, we are going to reposition ourselves on the other side of the somatic lens and look through it from the other end—from the inside looking out—so we can understand how your mind-body sees the world. Or more specifically, we will try to understand how your *anxious* mind-body sees the world.

The point of contact between your internal world and the external world is your lens, your perception—how you see reality. But what you see is a whole-body experience, not just a visual one. Perception is the active unfolding of a neural process that is continually integrating information received from your five senses— touch, taste, sight, hearing, and smell—in order to organize, interpret, and make sense of the world around you. Perception is thus not only how you see the world (for example, a person, relationship, situation, or circumstance), but also how you understand, make meaning of, and experience the world.

Your perceptual system also helps you see and experience the world as constant and stable, despite the ever-changing stream of sensory information flowing into the system. However, seeing the external world as steady and stable is possible only when your internal world is steady and stable. If your internal world is dysregulated or if it is easily activated and variable, then your perception of the external world is going to reflect that. When old, unresolved fears continually rattle your nervous system and keep you primed for the worst, then your perception of reality is going to be that the worst is coming. And when you expect the worst, you are going to focus your attention on those things that support this expectation, so that you are not caught off guard. Such focus will create a perception of the world as a dicey, unreliable place demanding constant hypervigilance and precaution to ensure your safety and survival. But what would imbue your perceptual lens with such fear and distrust? Once again, we return to implicit memory to answer this question.

Then and When versus Here and Now

Your perceptual system is continually integrating incoming sensory information with right and left hemispheric ways of knowing and understanding. Combining logic and reason with intuitive, felt-sense knowing enables you to maintain a steady and fluid perception of reality despite its being in constant flux. However, for the anxious mind-body, perception is often distorted, much like a funhouse mirror. This is because the implicit memory of unresolved fear that informs your sensory system is causing you to interpret sensory signals as dangerous or threatening, which then informs how you see and experience reality.

Let's pause for a recap. The right hemisphere, with its strong connection to the brain stem and the limbic system, is in charge of unconscious, emotional processing of present-moment experience. It does this, in part, by consulting implicit body memory and measuring it against the current situation or circumstance. In a split second, the right hemisphere scans the present moment, detects similarities between the past and present, and locks into that which appears familiar or the same. It will also eliminate novel information that is too different or that doesn't fit into your existing schema of past experience. This is how your mind-body makes sense of the present moment—by comparing it to the past. If you notice, this process does not include a logical assessment of the current situation or circumstance. Only after the limbic system has attached emotional meaning to the incoming sensory information does it then dispatch its findings to higher cortical areas for a more thoughtful assessment. However, for the anxious mind-body, rational, objective assessment is often fragmented, distorted, or hijacked altogether.

If the limbic structures conclude that the incoming sensory information indicates threat or danger, then, with the help of the brain stem, they will preempt logical evaluation of the present moment—an evaluation that could prevent a reactive response. When this happens, they will inhibit your ability to distinguish the past from the present, causing you to respond to the present as if it were the past. And so, for the anxious mind-body, perception is often a *then-and-when experience,* not a *here-and-now experience.*

Let's shift our focus and take a peek into the way your personal narratives influence your perceptions. This will allow you to see how your past is reflected in your perceptions. It will also help you orient to a system of understanding your perceptions that will make it easier to challenge them.

Perceptions and Personal Narratives

The somatic lens tells us that *anxiety is a state of present-moment fear based on past experiences that are informing our expectations of future events.* This definition of anxiety implies a skewed perception of reality, with split focus on the past and the future. This is because the unresolved fear and stress from past experiences tell the anxious mind-body that the world is unsafe, unpredictable, and untrustworthy and to be on high alert should the bad thing happen again in the future. As a result, the anxious mind-body regularly consults the past in order to predict the future so as to ensure successful adaptation to the current situation or circumstance. As you can see, inherent in this perception of reality is the expectation that the past will repeat itself: that *what has been is what will be.* When you consider this, you can begin to see how your personal narrative is reflected in your perceptions and how your perceptions can, very surreptitiously, end up creating the reality you fear most.

Recall the personal narratives you uncovered in the previous exercises. Notice that the key organizing principles of those narratives are *expectation* and *predictability*—*If this, then that.* Now, recall the core beliefs around which those narratives are woven and the thought patterns they generate. Notice how these core beliefs reflect your perceptions of yourself and the world and how the thought patterns that emerge from them guide your choices and behaviors; they guide the way you engage people, situations, and circumstances in your life.

Now, the thing about perceptions is that there is a reciprocal component to them. Perception is a process of understanding the world, making meaning of the world, *and* experiencing the world. When you believe certain things about the world and experience it a certain way, you are going to engage it accordingly. In other words, if you experience the world (for example, a person, relationship, situation, or circumstance) as unsafe and untrustworthy, you will treat the world as such. And when you treat the world as unsafe and untrustworthy, the world tends to respond according to your treatment of it. That is, you elicit the response you are expecting, which then creates a situation where you are living the future you expect. This process reinforces your faulty perceptions, and therefore your anxiety. Challenging your perceptions, then, becomes an integral part of regulating your fear response and reducing your anxiety as well as creating the change you want in your life.

Challenging Perceptions

This is a simple exercise intended to give you a general sense of how perception is linked with your mind and body. Additionally, it illustrates the resistance you can experience when you try to challenge your perceptions to see things in a more accurate or favorable way.

Take a brief moment to recall a time in the recent past when your anxiety was activated or a time during which you were upset (sad, mad, disappointed, etc.). Now, challenge yourself to see this situation from a different, more positive angle—perhaps from the other person's perspective or from a perspective where a more favorable outcome is likely. Now, SOAR—sense, observe, articulate, and reflect. Notice how your body responds. What sensations are you aware of? What are the first thoughts that pop into your mind? Do those thoughts reflect your narrative and core beliefs? Is there resistance to this new perception? If so, why?

To help illustrate the power of perception, I will introduce you to my client Grace. Grace has a beautiful heart and a fighting spirit. She is fierce and she is loyal—if she takes you into her circle, you have a friend for life. She will faithfully have your back when you need support, she will give you the last penny in her purse if times get rough, and she will throw herself on a grenade to save your life. Grace is someone you want in your corner. And yet, as tough as she was, no one would ever have guessed that Grace suffered from chronic anxiety. Grace's anxiety impacted many aspects of her life, including her relationships with her husband and her adolescent children. Specifically, Grace experienced anxiety when confronted with pushback from her kids because she anticipated a lack of support from her husband.

For example, one evening Grace's daughter asked to spend the night at her friend's house. Because it was a school night, Grace said no. Needless to say, Grace's daughter did not accept this answer without a fight. While her daughter tried to convince Grace how unreasonable she was being, Grace's husband, who was standing nearby, was silent during the conflict. It wasn't until Grace gave him "the look" that her husband chimed in and said to their daughter, "Listen to your mother," at which point their daughter rolled her eyes and stomped off in defeat.

Later that evening, Grace shared with her husband how upset and disappointed she was that he didn't support her during the conflict with their daughter. Aghast, her husband said, "What are you talking about? I fully supported you!" "No, you didn't," Grace snapped. "You just stood there like a lump on a log. It wasn't until I eyeballed you that you chimed in." Her husband, completely baffled, replied, "I didn't say anything because I thought that any comment from me would escalate the situation." Grace was reasonable and knew her husband wasn't a liar, but she was also unconvinced that he was being supportive. This upset Grace and left her feeling uncertain about how to reconcile her perception of the sleepover incident with her husband's.

Grace processed with me her struggle to resolve the clash of perceptions. She knew her husband was being honest when he said he supported her parenting decision. But to Grace, her husband's behavior didn't feel like support, it felt like abandonment. It felt like her husband had hung her out to dry. I mentioned to Grace that perhaps the kind of support she needed from him was greater verbal participation in conflicts with their children. She agreed that would be helpful, but she still couldn't shake the feeling that he was unsupportive in her time of need. I then reflected back to Grace that perhaps what she couldn't shake was her *fear* that she couldn't trust him to have her back. Or, put differently, she *feared* believing her husband when he said he had her back.

As we began to consider this possibility, we looked at Grace's personal narratives and the belief system on which they were predicated. Among the narratives activated in this incident was: *If I need help, I will be let down.* The belief inherent in this narrative was: *I cannot count on anyone to have my back.* And the logical conclusion to this thought process was: *Therefore, I will be left alone to fight for myself.* At this point in our work, Grace also knew where her narratives came from.

Grace grew up in a family in which she experienced a lot of conflict with her mother, whom Grace described as "extremely unreasonable." In fact, Grace often felt that her mother would purposely upset Grace because she enjoyed the conflict. Making matters worse, her father, a pliant and passive man, would not stand up for Grace when her mother was being irrational. Each time she was embroiled in an argument with her mother, her father would stand by and watch, but never would he support Grace's appeals for fairness. Grace felt so hurt and let down by him that she often didn't know who she was more upset with, her mother or her father.

Using Mindful Somatic Awareness, Grace reflected on her personal narratives and the historical experiences from which they emerged. As she did this, she noticed parallels between the past and present events. Specifically, she noticed how, in the sleepover incident, she unconsciously perceived her daughter as being unreasonable like her mother. She also unconsciously perceived her husband as being passive like her father, which left Grace feeling powerless and without support during the conflict. The sensory experience of the sleepover incident was so similar to her experience as a child that her brain stem and limbic system had decided that it was, in fact, the very same experience. Her mind-body's interpretation, then, made her husband someone who could not be counted on. And because the fear and hurt from the original experiences remained unresolved in her nervous system, Grace could not take a risk to see her husband any other way. For Grace, holding onto her fear was a protective measure she could count on to mobilize defensive reactions that kept her from feeling overwhelmed and powerless. To take a risk and believe what she knew to be true—that her husband was not her father and that he was, in fact, reliable—made her much more vulnerable than she felt comfortable with. However, in order to alleviate her anxiety, that was exactly the risk she needed to take.

So how does Grace challenge her perceptions in a way that allows her to acknowledge and honor her past experience as it shows up in the present moment, while changing the way she sees the present moment? How does she allow herself to trust that her husband will have her back?

Cultivating Dual Awareness

The answer to this question is to cultivate dual awareness (Rothschild 2000). Dual awareness is the ability to have conscious awareness in two places at the same time. That is, to be consciously aware that your implicit memory has been activated and your body is having a *then-and-when experience* while simultaneously being consciously aware that you are in the present moment having a *here-and-now experience*. This is very different from an anxious mindset with split attention on the past and the future. In fact, dual awareness is a present-moment experience in which you are simply aware of the past showing up in the present while holding awareness that the present is not the past.

When you practice dual awareness, you create the opportunity to challenge faulty perceptions and work through the anxiety that keeps you experiencing the world as dangerous and threatening. With mindful focus on your feelings and body sensations, you become conscious of yourself as an *experiencer* of the past implicit memory that has been activated. However, at the very same time, by orienting yourself to the external environment, you can become conscious of yourself as an *observer* of what you are experiencing in the present (Rothschild 2000). With dual awareness of yourself as both an *experiencer* and an *observer,* you can see reality from both perspectives. You can then use your observing self (left hemisphere) to challenge the perceptions influenced by the fear and anxiety coming from your experiencing self (right hemisphere). In this way, dual awareness facilitates right and left hemisphere participation in your perceptual unfolding, creating the opportunity to challenge your old lens and see things with new eyes. Over time, dual awareness will strengthen your perceptual objectivity while allowing you to remain connected to your subjective felt-sense experience.

What follows is an exercise that uses Mindful Somatic Awareness and SOAR to help you cultivate dual awareness. As you engage in the exercise, remember that if you feel your nervous system getting too activated, pause the exercise and return to a resourcing, grounding, or orienting exercise from chapter 3. This will help you bring your nervous system back into a state of regulation so you can complete the exercise. If your activation persists, stop the exercise altogether and return to it when you feel more strength and resiliency to engage in it.

Then and When, Here and Now

Find a quiet place where you will not be disturbed. Take a moment to recall a recent time when your anxiety was activated or a time when you were upset. If you would like, you can use the same incident from the first exercise in this chapter. Now, close your eyes and bring your awareness to your breath. Then expand your awareness to the rest of your body. Once you are grounded in your body, SOAR—sense, observe, articulate, and reflect. As you SOAR, be mindful that the sensations you feel vibrating in your body are generated by implicit memory activation. That is, your body is remembering a "then and when" experience.

As you SOAR and articulate aloud the sensations you are experiencing, prepare to bring your awareness to your immediate environment. When you feel ready, gradually open your eyes and orient to the space around you by scanning the room and naming the objects you see. As you anchor yourself in the present moment, note that you are having a "here and now" experience *and* that there is nothing to fear.

Next, shift into dual awareness—awareness of yourself experiencing the somatic sensations of past memories and of yourself observing the space around you in the present moment. Over the next few moments, slowly alternate your attention between your internal world and your external world while holding awareness of both at the same time. It is helpful to articulate your dual awareness aloud. For example, "My legs feel antsy and my chest feels tight. My breath is a bit shallow. I also see the blue armchair across the room and the glass vase on the counter. This tells me I am right here, right now, and that I am okay."

When you are finished, be sure to bring your attention back to your breath and ground yourself in your body. Then make the "I" statement—"I am right here, right now, and I am okay."

Let's return to Grace to see how combining Mindful Somatic Awareness with dual awareness helped her challenge her perceptions and work through the fear that kept her from trusting her husband's support.

During session one day, I asked Grace to close her eyes and sit in Mindful Somatic Awareness while imagining the sleepover incident. I then guided her attention to the moment in the conflict with her daughter when she needed her husband's support but felt he wasn't there. As she connected to this moment and tracked her sensations, she began to experience symptoms of a fear response—accelerated heart rate, pit in her stomach, and tightness in her throat. I then asked Grace to slowly open her eyes and bring her attention to her feet, feeling the support of the ground beneath them. Once she had connected to the ground, I invited Grace to gradually scan the room, naming aloud the objects she saw. Next, I asked Grace if she could hold dual awareness of herself in her present surroundings and, at the same time, her physiological experience of the past.

Grace remarked that though she was aware of the historical fear her body was experiencing, she was also aware that she was in the present time and that she was not actually in danger.

As Grace held dual awareness, her nervous system settled a bit, creating an opportunity to challenge her perception. I asked her to return to the sleepover incident and, instead of *feeling her husband's absence,* I invited her to imagine *feeling his presence,* that he was standing there in support of her. In other words, I asked her to actively change her perception and imagine that, in that moment, he had her back. Once again, Grace's body began to demonstrate symptoms of fear. And once again I brought her attention to the external space around her. As Grace was able to come back into the present moment, she could reflect on the fear she was still experiencing in her body as a response to challenging her original perception.

Throughout the session, Grace continued to challenge her perception using dual awareness. At first, Grace's mind-body experienced considerable fear and resistance to changing her perception. "It is very hard to do. It feels too risky." "What feels risky about it?" I asked. Grace thought long and hard about my inquiry. "I don't have a logical explanation. I am just afraid of the outcome if I do." I decided to try a different angle and asked Grace what it was like for her when she would argue with her mother. "It was awful. Nothing I did, nothing I said had an impact. She was unmovable. I was utterly powerless and alone in it." As Grace spoke, her body began to tremble and her throat tightened. I invited her to allow the sensations to move through her. As she did, her resistance softened and her eyes began to fill with tears. Through her tears, Grace explained that if she accepted the new perception and believed that her husband was reliable and had her back, then what rose to the surface was all of the feelings she had had during those experiences with her mother and father—the anger, fear, and powerlessness she had felt with her mother and the feelings of betrayal she had felt with her father, who was supposed to protect her. Grace's old perception safeguarded her from reexperiencing these feelings, but it perpetuated her anxiety. This is because her old lens kept her seeing others as unreliable and kept her nervous system stuck in past experiences where she felt powerless and alone.

Grace's fear of emotional pain and stress is very common. Most often, anxiety is not just the fear of something terrible happening in the world around you, but the fear of *feeling* something terrible in the world within you. Anxiety includes the fear of reexperiencing the same dreadful, overwhelming feelings you had during the original frightening experiences *and* being alone and powerless with that fear. Remember, as children, when our little nervous system is flooded with big and unpleasant emotions, our body is overwhelmed and our mind is confused. Likewise with teenagers, whose emotional sensitivity often outpaces their ability to process and understand their emotional reactions (Siegel 2013). So for a child or adolescent who did not have adequate or reliable comfort and support from a loving adult, this feeling of being emotionally overwhelmed can be a very scary experience. Such was the case with Grace, who feared the arguments with her mother *and* the surge of terrible emotions they would trigger.

The following is an exercise to help you cultivate dual awareness and challenge faulty perceptions. It does this by taking your negative core *beliefs* and contrasting them with what you *know* to be true, what you *know* is a more reasoned perception. Consider it like this: Simply stated, you "know" with your left hemisphere and you "believe" with your right hemisphere. So your logical and objective left hemisphere *knows* there is nothing to fear. But your right hemisphere does not *believe* this to be true. This is because your right hemisphere carries the truth of your subjective experience, and your subjective experiences have shown you that the world is unsafe. So you do not believe that there is nothing to fear. That is, *you do not believe what you know.* This exercise is intended to integrate your right and left hemispheres in order to help you believe what you know, so you can begin to feel more empowered and see the world around you as less scary and more responsive to you and your efforts to influence it.

To Know, Perhaps to Believe

Return to the negative core beliefs in chapter 5. Choose one that resonates with you in this moment and write it on a piece of paper. For example, *I believe I am powerless and alone.* Now, next to the negative belief, write down the opposite of that belief. However, when you write down the opposite, positive belief, it is important to write it the following way: *I believe such and such. But I know such and such.* For example: *I believe I am powerless and alone. But I know I am strong, capable, and supported by others.*

Now, make a list of memories or occasions when you experienced what you know—when you experienced the opposite of what your negative core belief tells you. For instance, using the example above, you would make a list of times when you experienced strength, capability, and support from others. Once you have made this list, repeat the statement: "I believe… But I know…" and then add: "I know this because…" For example: "I believe I am powerless and alone. But I know I am strong, capable, and supported by others. I know this because when I was afraid of stating my opinion, I spoke up anyway. With the support of Sally, I stepped forward and said my piece."

Once you have your statement completed—"I believe… But I know… I know this because…"—sit in a chair in a quiet room. With your feet flat on the floor, bring your attention to your breath and then expand your attention to the rest of your body. Now, say the statement aloud and SOAR. Notice what sensations come to life in your body. Notice any sensations that indicate resistance. Notice sensations that indicate a sense of relief.

This exercise is important because it trains your mind to see significant aspects of your experience that your fear obscures. Remember, the anxious mind-body looks for evidence to support its belief that we have reason to fear, worry, or be in doubt. In light of this, you will likely experience your beliefs trying to invalidate what you know, in an effort to preserve your existing defense system and ensure your safety. I call this the "Yes, But effect." The "Yes, But effect" is a response intended to invalidate the truth of what you know. We all have this voice within us that tries to sabotage our efforts to change our beliefs and perceptions. During this exercise, it will look something like this: "I believe I am powerless and alone. But I know I am strong, capable, and supported by others. I know this because when I was afraid of stating my opinion, I spoke up anyway. With the support of Sally, I stepped forward and said my piece. *Yes, that may be true, but* I am not as strong as Sally and there was that time when…"

If you experience the "Yes, But effect," simply recognize it, name it, and honor its genuine intention to protect your safety and well-being. Then gently challenge it by bringing your awareness back to what you know to be true. As you do this, SOAR—challenge the resistance on a body level and work to integrate what you *know* into your somatic self.

Tip: The next time your anxiety gets triggered, identify what you are *believing* about the present moment. Then challenge your belief with what you *know* about certain people or aspects of the situation or circumstance. This is a helpful way to change your perceptions and remove the historical debris that distorts your perceptual lens.

In the next chapter we will continue to use the somatic lens to link your internal experience with your external experience in order to deepen your understanding of how your anxiety influences your perceptions and behavior. Specifically, we will focus our attention on the way in which your anxiety impacts your ability to set healthy boundaries that safeguard your emotional and physical self, while allowing you to remain open and available to others. We will use what we have learned so far to gain insight into how early boundary-setting experiences have created anxiety about communicating your needs, which makes it difficult for you to draw and negotiate appropriate limits as an adult.

CHAPTER 7

Anxiety and Boundaries

As we continue to look through the somatic lens at the world around us to enhance our understanding of how the anxious mind-body experiences reality, we come to see that there are a myriad of external sources of anxiety. Among the most common of these sources is the ongoing, ever-present need to set steady and reliable boundaries. Protecting your internal world (your thoughts, feelings, needs, and desires) and your external world (your physical space and body) is a daunting task. The task is even harder when your early experiences of boundary-setting carry with them fears of loss, disapproval, or disregard. In the following pages we will explore the origins of your current boundary-setting patterns so you can understand your struggle to draw limits and assert your needs. Additionally, you will glean insight into the somatic nature of boundaries and fine-tune your ability to recognize and interpret your body's cues that signal the need to draw protective barriers. In doing so, you will enhance your facility in setting boundaries so you can freely open your heart and trust that you can (and will) step forward and draw the line when necessary.

Drawing boundaries is a profoundly life-affirming skill set that facilitates your ability to protect your physical and energetic space. Like the bank of a river or the shoreline of the ocean, boundaries draw a clear line between what is you and what is not you; they define where *you* end and *other* begins. In doing so, boundaries enable the authentic unfolding of your truest self. They safeguard you against being overwhelmed; they protect you against the absorption of harmful emotional debris from others; and they shield you against the disregard of those who do not respect your sacred right to expand, express, and create. When you trust in your ability to draw clear and effective boundaries, you can freely engage the world without fear because you are no longer at the whim and mercy of whatever and whomever comes your way. You can take command of your life and decide who and what is given access to your heart and who and what is not—and why.

It is important to note that boundaries are intended not only to protect you, but to protect others as well. Boundaries safeguard the important people in your life against the resentment often experienced when you feel used and mistreated. When you learn to assert limits, you will find that your relationships improve because you can show up and be present for others in a way that meets their needs *and* yours. You can give to others, care for others, sacrifice for others, and love others because the locus of power remains within you—it is *your* choice how much you give and where you draw the line. Even when you negotiate boundaries in your relationships, you can sit at the table as an active participant and advocate for your own needs while respecting the needs of others. In doing so, you can settle on a boundary that respects everyone involved, including yourself.

Many times, however, boundaries are not experienced by others as respectful or beneficial. Not everyone responds well to hearing the word *No*. Boundaries are often perceived as hurtful, attacking, or controlling. The protective limits we set are thus frequently met with defensiveness or rebuke. This makes drawing the line very difficult and anxiety provoking. Making boundary-setting even harder is our own tendency to project our emotional injuries onto others, believing they will experience our *No's* the way we might experience theirs—as hurtful, attacking, or controlling. Because we don't want to perpetrate emotional pain, we absorb responsibility for everyone's feelings and consent to a series of *Yeses* that end up making us feel used, overwhelmed, and resentful. This is why it is essential to understand your early boundary-setting experiences—so you can work through the anxiety that keeps you from setting effective limits with others *and* accept and respect the boundaries others set with you without taking it personally. Later in the chapter we will expand on the implicit fears that influence your boundary-setting style. First, however, it is important to establish a basic understanding of the different types of boundaries.

The Two Different Boundary Types: Internal and External

Generally speaking, there are two types of boundaries—internal and external. Internal boundaries refer to the dynamic processes of your internal world, such as thoughts, feelings, needs, and desires. Effective internal boundaries support your psychological and emotional health by screening incoming data and granting access only to information that facilitates your personal growth and aligns you with your authentic self. Further, the parameters that protect your internal world help you distinguish your thoughts, feelings, and emotions from others'. When your nervous system is activated with anxiety, it becomes increasingly difficult to differentiate your intellectual and emotional self from that of others. When this happens, you are vulnerable to those who want to convince you that you should think and feel the way they do because your point of view is not in their best interest. Internal boundaries keep you identified with your core self so you can assert your needs even when you are stressed and overwhelmed.

The opposite is also true. That is, your internal boundary system keeps *you* in check, allowing others to have their own experience without you trying to align them with your point of view. With good internal boundaries, you do not feel threatened by perceptions of reality that differ from your own. Rather, you can safely hold onto your own self while still being able to hear, validate, and empathize with the experience of others. Reliable internal boundaries maintain the differences that separate you and make you unique while preserving the emotional connection that bonds you to those you love and like.

Finally, strong internal boundaries facilitate personal ownership of your thoughts, feelings, and needs. They hold you accountable for your choices, disallowing you from blaming others for how you think and feel or for the circumstances of your life. As an extension, when you claim responsibility for keeping your side of the street clean, you no longer assume others' responsibility to do the same. That is, you can support others and have compassion for them without doing their work and shouldering their emotional burdens. In this way, healthy internal boundaries enhance closeness and intimacy in your relationships by creating a safe space to be open and vulnerable.

If internal boundaries protect your inner world, then external boundaries protect your outer world—your physical body and space. External boundaries define your physical property line and determine how close or distant you are or want to be from those around you. External boundaries can extend beyond your actual physical body, outlining a personal zone that facilitates comfort when sharing space with others. Depending on whom you are sharing space with, this personal zone can extend several inches to several feet. The parameters that protect your physical space also regulate touching and being touched. They inform you and others when it is okay to make physical contact and when it is not. They also let you and others know what kind of physical contact is acceptable.

Beyond physical proximity and touch, your external boundary extends to your personal property—your purse, wallet, closet, mail, computer, cell phone, or other things of that nature. Attributes of your inner world take physical expression in your belongings and the contents of your personal space. When these external boundaries have been violated without your consent, it is an invasion of privacy where you can feel tremendously exposed and vulnerable. As with internal boundaries, when you have steady and reliable external boundaries, you are more mindful and respectful of others' external boundaries. Further, the safety experienced when you and others have a healthy boundary system fosters respectful and trustworthy relationships in which you feel safe to express yourself freely and authentically.

The Four Different Boundary-Setting Styles

Now that you are more familiar with the two types of boundaries, let's briefly review the different styles of boundary-setting. Knowing what kind of boundary you are working with—internal or external—is one thing, but how you set those boundaries is another thing altogether. How you draw the line is referred to as your *boundary-setting style* and reflects what your boundaries typically look like. That is, do your boundaries generally look like a chain-link fence or do they look like a wall of cinder blocks? Are they porous and easy to get through or are they impenetrable, like a fortress? The following is a brief description of the four different types of boundary-setting styles. As you read through them, note what style resonates most with you and what your boundaries generally look like.

There are four basic styles of boundary-setting: loose, rigid, oscillating, and flexible.

Loose Boundaries

Loose boundaries are very blurred and indistinct. They reflect a tendency to say *Yes*, even when you want to say *No*. Loose boundaries thus provide very little protection against incoming demands, which can be both overwhelming and draining. The fear of saying *No* often comes from a sense of responsibility or obligation to take care of others. Thus, if you have loose boundaries, you tend to prioritize others above yourself and struggle to differentiate your own needs from the needs of those around you. Additionally, loose boundaries can emerge from fears of rejection or abandonment. When you fear that your boundary will upset others and that they will respond by retaliating in some hurtful way, you will choose to comply with their requests to avoid ruffling feathers and keep the flock together.

When your tendency is to communicate a *loose No*, it may also be that you are sensitive to others' asserting a *firm No* to you. You may wince and take it personally when they draw boundaries with you. In fact, you may not always be aware of others' boundaries and unintentionally breach their personal limits. This can be experienced by others as intrusive and elicit feedback you are not expecting. Because loose boundaries do not adequately draw the line that separates *you* from *other*, it is difficult to hold onto a felt sense of self and to know who you are, what you want, and what you need. And while having loose boundaries can make you wonderfully sensitive and attuned to the needs of others, you are also at great risk for becoming overwhelmed and experiencing ongoing anxiety because you cannot reliably establish parameters that protect your heart and support your interests.

Rigid Boundaries

If loose boundaries reflect a tendency to say *Yes*, then rigid boundaries reflect a tendency to say *No*. Such boundaries are impenetrable, with no access gates that allow others in or that allow you out. They fiercely protect your privacy, allowing you to hold your cards close to your chest and to play only those cards you want others to see. Such privacy can be very isolating and lonely and inhibit closeness and intimacy. However, this is by design as those with rigid boundaries tend to experience closeness and vulnerability as unsafe and invasive.

Because rigid boundaries restrict access to others and enforce strict rules of engagement, those who draw hard lines tend to be very independent and self-reliant—asking for help is not in their repertoire. And while these qualities can yield great benefits, they also tend to keep you at a distance from others. You may thus be perceived as guarded and emotionally aloof or unavailable. The ability to draw firm boundaries has the value of protecting you from the influence of others' thoughts and feelings, keeping you connected to your core self. However, the anxiety you experience in saying *Yes* ultimately restricts the breadth of potential for personal fulfillment, inhibiting a sense of joy and pleasure that comes with shared experiences.

Oscillating Boundaries

Oscillating boundaries are those that move back and forth between loose and rigid. If your boundary style oscillates, you tend to carry the fears and attributes of those who struggle to say *Yes* in addition to the fears and attributes of those who struggle to say *No*. This oscillating boundary style often reflects a reactive response to fears of openness and vulnerability as well as to fears of closedness and isolation: there is a general confusion as to where to draw the line.

Those who oscillate between loose and rigid boundary styles have a longing to feel open and connected, to be helpful and pleasing, but when the contact feels too close or the demands feel too immense, the vulnerability in being open becomes overwhelming. This triggers a fear response, eliciting a reaction that severs the connection—you draw a firm and rigid boundary and disconnect. However, the comfort initially experienced in the disconnect is short-lived; it's too lonely and there are fears of losing others. So the rigidity loosens and the door reopens. The oscillating boundary can be very disorienting and anxiety provoking; the attunement with your felt sense feels unreliable and the inner voice that guides your sense of safety is muted, making it very difficult to know when and where to set limits.

Flexible Boundaries

Flexible boundaries are closed enough to be protective, but open enough to let others in. Those with a flexible boundary style recognize the need for a boundary to be adaptable to various people and situations and are able to adjust the boundary according to their needs and preferences in each emerging moment. The ability to do this comes from a strong attunement to their felt sense of self as well as a healthy entitlement to say *No*—*and* a healthy entitlement to say *Yes*. Flexible boundaries facilitate closeness and intimacy because they support heartful connections while standing guard against emotional coercion. Additionally, they encourage self-expansion and risk-taking because they protect against becoming overwhelmed. On the flip side, flexible boundaries encourage retreat when your mind-body is in need of peace and restoration; they champion guilt-free *No's* that insulate you from the persuasions of others and keep you identified with your core self.

Knowing My Boundary Style

Now that you have a general idea of the different types of boundaries and the different boundary-setting styles, take a moment to reflect on what your boundaries typically look like and write your reflections down.

First, close your eyes, take a few deep breaths, and bring your attention to your body. When you feel more body-aware, open your eyes. Begin to consider why it is you may draw boundaries this way. Think of different situations where it is more difficult for you to set limits than in others. Why might this be? Recall how boundaries were set in your family and the formative environments in which you were raised. Were boundaries respected or were they ignored? How did you adapt to this? Think about a time in your past when you tried to set a boundary or wanted to say *No*, but it was unsuccessful. What impact did this have on you? Think of a time when you asserted your needs and your boundary was respected. What effect did this have on you? If you would like to change how you presently set boundaries, what would you like your boundary-setting style to look like? What are the fears that keep you from doing this? How do your negative thoughts and core beliefs inform your boundary-setting style?

As you allow your mind to consider the origins of your boundary-setting style and your present relationship with boundaries, SOAR—sense the vibrations of your somatic self, observe and articulate your experience of these vibrations, and reflect on the possible origins of these sensations. What would cause your body to respond this way? Notice what happens in your somatic self as you recall memories of setting boundaries. Pay attention to what happens when you consider setting boundaries differently.

Acquainting yourself with the way your body recorded memories of early boundary-setting experiences will help you work through the fear that keeps you from honoring your needs and preferences in the present time. Further, establishing awareness of how your mind and body respond to one another around boundary-setting is an important first step in regulating the anxiety you experience when you assert your needs and draw parameters around your internal and external world.

To illustrate how boundary-setting can generate anxiety, I will introduce you to my client Jenny. Jenny struggled mightily to assert her needs and establish boundaries in all aspects of her life. So much so that, when I met her, she had created for herself a life that accommodated her fear of setting limits with others. That is, she avoided boundary-setting altogether. Routinized and predictable, Jenny's daily activities minimized, to the fullest extent possible, occasions that would require her to say *No*. However, her life was so controlled that it also minimized occasions for her to say *Yes*. This was because saying *Yes* to new experiences would, at some point, require her to draw a boundary and say *No*. Fearful of saying *Yes* and *No*, Jenny felt imprisoned by her life. Shackled by her anxiety, she was unable to move toward the thing she wanted most—to fall in love. What Jenny desperately longed for was a committed relationship with someone she loved and admired; she wanted to share her life with someone whom she adored and who would adore her. However, loving companionship eluded Jenny because being in a relationship required the ability to set healthy and flexible boundaries, something she was fearful of doing.

Using the somatic lens, we explored the origins of Jenny's fears around setting boundaries. It didn't take us long to unearth the roots of her anxiety. Raised in a family whose boundaries were exceptionally loose, Jenny learned early on that setting limits around her internal and external space was not welcomed by her family. With her father largely absent, most of Jenny's young life was spent with her mother and her sister, who enlisted Jenny to gratify their needs and to accept their choices regardless of the impact on her. This left no room for Jenny to have any needs of her own. What made this confusing for young Jenny was that, despite this harmful dynamic, there was also a lot of love that bonded Jenny to her mother and her sister: they were very close. And so, to preserve the love and closeness, Jenny adapted to the boundary styles of her family without much ado. As a child, she unconsciously shut down her own needs and disconnected from her core self to become whatever it was her family needed her to be. Over time, she morphed into a consummate pleaser, able to anticipate the needs of her family and settle any emotional turbulence to keep the peace.

In her adaptation to the boundary style of her family, Jenny lost touch with her true self. She was so busy accommodating the needs of others and so fearful of drawing boundaries that she was no longer attuned to her felt sense of self—who she was, what she wanted, and what she needed. The degree to which her sense of self was impoverished was never so apparent as when she asked me one day, "Who should I be attracted to?" Taken aback, I hastily inquired, "What do you mean?" "I mean, who should I be attracted to for a relationship." Truly staggered, I didn't know how to answer this question and stumbled to reflect back what I thought might be the underlying issues embedded in her question. All I could think was, *I don't know. Attraction isn't really a choice—you just feel it when it happens.* But that was the problem for Jenny; she didn't feel it. She didn't feel what she desired; she only felt what others desired.

Jenny's story illustrates how our boundary style is informed by our early environment. As children, the important people in our life teach us how to honor our thoughts, needs, preferences, and desires by the way they respect the boundaries we set with them. They also teach us by the way they set *their* boundaries with *us*, as well as by showing us how to set boundaries with others. These experiences become wired into our somatic self and unconsciously influence the way we establish personal limits and assert our needs as adults. Jenny's story also illustrates the somatic nature of boundaries. Her story highlights how, when we are disconnected from our body or when anxiety thwarts our ability to accurately read somatic cues that indicate a need for a boundary, we are without a compass to guide our efforts to draw that boundary. When this happens, our boundary-setting becomes a reactive or habitual response rather than an embodied and mindful one.

The Somatic Nature of Boundaries

Boundaries are, first and foremost, a sensory experience. The ability to step forward and speak on your own behalf emerges from an instinctive felt-sense awareness that the integrity of yourself is at risk and a protective line needs to be communicated to warn others not to violate your internal or external space. This felt sense comes in the form of sensations. There are a variety of different sensations or cues the body uses to communicate that a boundary is required, or that one has been breached: uneasiness in your stomach, general stiffening in your body, tension in your shoulders, tightening of your jaw, restricted breathing, impulse to lean back or walk away, avoiding eye contact, and feelings of agitation, irritation, or annoyance. The list is long and varied and unique to each individual. Your work is to acquaint yourself with your own felt-sense experience of setting boundaries to identify when your boundaries have been trespassed.

The following exercises are intended to increase your awareness of the unique signals your body uses to communicate the need for a boundary. These exercises foster awareness of somatic alerts to boundary violations or potential violations. When you are well attuned to your body's boundary signals and can consciously identify them as such, you are connected to your internal warning system specifically designed to protect you.

Saying No

Find a quiet space where you will not be disrupted. Begin by closing your eyes and bringing your attention first to your breath and then to the rest of your body. When you feel more body-aware, open your eyes. Stand with your feet shoulder width apart and your knees slightly bent to ensure they are not locked. Now, one at a time, enact each of the following prompts. After each prompt, pause and SOAR. If you need to sit after each prompt in order to best facilitate SOAR, I encourage you to do so. When you are ready, stand and resume with the prompts.

Prompts:

1. Make a stop signal with your hand.

2. Make a stop signal with your hand and say *No*.

3. Cross your arms in front of your chest.

4. Cross your arms in front of your chest and then turn your body away or walk away.

5. Lean back and away with your body.

6. Lean back and away with your head.

7. Using your facial expressions, frown, sneer, scowl, or grimace.

8. Tighten or clench your jaw.

9. Tighten or clench your jaw, show your teeth, and growl.

10. Raise both arms, hands in the shape of a stop sign, and imagine pushing away.

11. Raise both arms, hands in the shape of a stop sign, and say *Stop.*

12. Narrow your eyes and glare.

13. Pretend you are avoiding eye contact.

14. Clench your fists.

As you SOAR, note what it felt like to say *No.* Did it feel empowering? Liberating? Uncomfortable? Confusing? Also, return to the reflective prompts in the previous exercise: Think of situations where it is difficult for you to set limits and why this might be. Recall how boundaries were set in your family or the environment in which you were raised. Think about a time in your past when you tried to set a boundary and it was unsuccessful. How did this impact you? What are the fears that keep you from setting more effective boundaries? How do your negative thoughts and core beliefs inform your boundary-setting style?

Helpful Tips:

- Try this exercise in front of a mirror. Sometimes the stimulus of seeing yourself set boundaries can generate deeper implicit memory activation that can yield greater insight into your anxiety around setting boundaries. However, should you try this exercise in front of a mirror and it is either distracting or activates you beyond what feels comfortable, step away from the mirror. The exercise is still effective without the visual stimulus.

- Place a chair in front of you. Now imagine a person with whom you struggle to set boundaries sitting in the chair. (It may help to put a pillow or an object in the chair that represents this person to help facilitate your imagination.) As you imagine this person, practice the prompts listed above and notice what happens in your body.

- As you enact each prompt, should you experience an impulse to add to the boundary-setting behavior, honor your impulse and do it. Your body is telling you it needs to do something in order to work through the fear that inhibits your ability to set effective boundaries.

Sensing *No*

Find a quiet space free from distraction. Sit with your feet flat on the ground. Close your eyes and bring your attention to your breath and then to your body. When you feel more body-aware, open your eyes. As above, enact each of the following prompts one at a time. After each prompt, pause and SOAR.

Imagine:

1. Being stared at.

2. Being glared at.

3. Being ogled at.

4. Someone standing too close to you (for example, in line at a store or at a social gathering).

5. Someone sitting too close to you.

6. Someone talking too close to your face.

7. Someone speaking "at" you in a condescending or derogatory tone.

8. Someone brushing up against you.

9. Forced physical contact (for example, a hug, handhold, sitting in someone's lap or someone sitting in yours).

10. Someone grabbing your wrist or arm.

As you SOAR after each prompt, enact the reflective prompts in the previous exercise to facilitate deeper insight into your somatic boundary-setting cues.

My Dance Space, Your Dance Space

This exercise uses your imagination to explore what it is like for you to draw healthy internal boundaries in your interpersonal relationships— boundaries that create space for each of you to express yourselves. As always, start by grounding yourself in your body by closing your eyes, bringing your attention to your breath and then to your body.

When you are ready, open your eyes and consider the following questions:

1. Think about a time when you had a conflict with someone you cared about. Perhaps they expressed a different opinion or belief than you. Perhaps there was a communication breakdown and a subsequent misunderstanding.

2. Next, SOAR: sense, observe, and then articulate aloud the sensations that vibrate in your body as you consider the conflict. Track these sensations for a while to see if they move or come to life in different parts of your body. Note also if the sensations themselves change (for example, tightness in chest to tingling in hands and feet).

3. Imagine setting a flexible internal boundary that acknowl-edges and honors the difference in thoughts, beliefs, and feelings. Notice what happens in your body as you set this boundary.

4. Imagine how your flexible boundary could bring about a resolution to the conflict where both of you feel understood and validated. Notice how your body responds to this outcome.

Let's return to Jenny to see how she used Mindful Somatic Awareness to work through early fears of boundary-setting to reclaim her life and fulfill her desire to fall in love. Jenny is an amazing soul. A gifted artist with a warm and expansive heart, what Jenny wanted more than anything was a companion with whom she could share her life. Jenny had so much joy and love to give, but no one to give it to because her fear of setting boundaries precluded any opportunity for new experiences, let alone a love relationship. Our work was to uncover the implicit memories associated with early boundary-setting experiences so she could work through her anxiety around drawing limits and actualize her deepest desire to experience love and fulfillment in a relationship.

Though Jenny grew up in a home with extremely loose boundaries, her own boundary style was notably rigid. Why might this be? To answer this question, I asked Jenny if she would be willing to engage in an exercise intended to reveal implicit memories from her childhood that might help us understand and assuage her anxiety. She readily agreed.

I asked Jenny to close her eyes and bring her attention to her body. Once she was grounded and more somatically aware, I asked her to imagine herself in a romantic relationship. Within an instant, she cringed—her entire body contracted and pulled itself in tight. "Can you tell me what you feel happening?" I asked. "Blech. I can't. It's way too much," she responded. Jenny's reaction was very strong and very immediate. Further, she quickly tried to cut off her sensations by contracting her body. This told me that her fear must be big and deep. Since she was not yet able to stay with her sensations for too long without becoming overwhelmed, I oriented Jenny's attention to the space around her to bring her back into the present moment. After naming aloud a few objects that caught her sight, Jenny brought her attention back to me and sat in quiet contemplation over what had happened. After a few moments, without any prompting, she said, "The minute I imagined myself with someone, I felt like I lost myself. Like I wasn't allowed to have my quirky habits, my individual wants, or my own opinions. I felt I had to be whatever they wanted me to be, as if I didn't matter, or I didn't exist."

For Jenny, to be in a relationship meant a complete loss of self— no boundaries whatsoever that would separate *her* from *other.* Jenny's implicit memories revealed that she unconsciously believed she had to forsake her own needs and wants for the needs and wants of others. And if she didn't comply with these demands, she would lose the attachment to the people she loved and depended on, and she would be all alone. This was her childhood felt predicament: lose myself or lose love. For a child, there is nothing more terrifying than the loss or threat of loss of those you need and love. So Jenny chose to let go of herself to preserve the love and attachment with her family. However, because these early implicit fears were never worked through, they remained in her somatic memory and the predicament she felt as a child unconsciously persisted as an adult. Only, as an adult, with no relationship to lose, Jenny was now fearful of losing herself.

As we continued to uncover her implicit memory and cultivate insight into her rigid boundary style, it became evident that the loss of self Jenny experienced as a child felt just as scary as the loss of love. To lose herself rendered her powerless and unable to mobilize authentic self-expression in reaction to what she saw happening around her and to her. Powerless and without a voice, Jenny was unable to protect herself when she felt scared, unable to defend herself when she felt mad, and unable to cry her tears when she felt sad. Believing this was her plight as an adult, Jenny renounced the loose boundary style she grew up with and adopted a rigid boundary style. Although her new boundary system precluded meaningful love relationships, at least she could hold onto herself and preserve control over her life. The only problem was, ultimately, Jenny was not happy. Her life remained empty and unfulfilled.

Over time, Jenny used Mindful Somatic Awareness to uncouple the sensory, emotional, and cognitive fragments that over-coupled love with loss of self and, conversely, the assertion of self (personal needs, wants, and opinions) with loss of love. We also challenged the unconscious core beliefs that emerged from this over-coupling, beliefs that told her she was not entitled to or deserving of having a fulfilling relationship in which she was appreciated and valued for who she was, as she was. As our work progressed, she connected to the indwelling entitlement to life that gave her permission to reclaim her right to authentic self-expression. In doing so, she learned to draw effective, life-affirming boundaries that protected her needs, wants, and desires without fearing that this would cause her to lose love.

As Jenny's story illustrates, the ability to draw boundaries is a requisite skill set for the preservation of self as well as the cultivation of healthy, loving relationships. Her story also highlights the influence of early boundary-setting experiences on our present ability to set limits with others. It helps us see how, during our formative years, the relationships with those we love and need profoundly inform how we regard ourselves and how our self-regard is expressed in our boundary-setting style. Beyond the importance of boundaries, however, Jenny's story brings to light the abiding desire we all have to build heartful relationships and share our life with others. Despite our deepest fears of closeness and vulnerability, there remains within us a persistent longing for meaningful connection. In the following chapter, we will use the somatic lens to look closer at our innate need for relationships and examine our instinct to move toward love and bonding. We also will untangle the various ways in which anxiety often interferes with closeness and intimacy and thwarts our instinctive efforts to turn to others for comfort, safety, and security when we are most in need.

CHAPTER 8

Anxiety and Relationships

We are profoundly relational beings. The drive we experience to build enduring and meaningful relationships and to feel safe and secure in those relationships is not accidental: it is an expression of our innate neurobiology. We are literally designed to connect and live in reciprocity with one another; our need for bonding and attachment is built into our very physiology. The implications of this are far reaching. However, in the following pages we will focus our attention on the ways in which relationships provide essential regulators for fear, fostering feelings of safety and security. We will take a closer look at your neurobiological design so you can clearly see how connecting with others is imperative to regulating your fear response and healing the deeper wounds that perpetuate your anxiety. We will also use Mindful Somatic Awareness to explore the origins of any unease and trepidation you may experience in turning to the important people in your life for comfort and support. Emotional ruptures in early bonding experiences remain stored in our implicit memory and keep us from leaning into our adult relationships for safety and reassurance. Identifying those early experiences will help you work through old fears of vulnerability so you can safely move toward connection with others and use those connections to experience lasting relief from your anxiety.

A defining feature of anxiety is a deficit in feeling safe, secure, and empowered. Also common to anxiety is a sense of being alone in your experience, without supportive and understanding others to be with you in your fear. When the absence of safety and security is coupled with feeling alone, your anxiety can become more acute (Badenoch 2018). This is because relationships provide the very resources we need to experience the safety and sense of belonging that bring our nervous system back into a state of regulation. Thus, when compassionate connection is missing or unavailable, so too are the vital resources your mind-body needs to settle and feel at peace.

Coregulation and the Social Engagement System

The ability to experience calmness and safety in relationships and social connections is called *coregulation,* and the system of neural resources that facilitates our ability to coregulate is called the *social engagement system* (Dana 2018). The social engagement system emerges from the *vagus nerve*—a major mind-body communicator woven into our parasympathetic nervous system. The vagus nerve works to regulate our physiological states by sending sensory information bi-directionally between the brain and body (Porges 2011). Mediated by the vagus nerve, the social engagement system facilitates anxiety reduction by searching for nonverbal cues of safety and danger in our interactions with others. For example, in the presence of another person, if our mind-body perceives their physiological gestures, facial expressions, vocal intonation, and eye contact as safe, and we experience a reciprocity and resonance with them, then our nervous system downregulates and our anxiety subsides. However, if our mind-body perceives their nonverbal communication as ambiguous or threatening, our nervous system will mobilize a protective response. Further, when our social engagement system joins with that of another person and there is a mutual exchange of safety cues, it creates a feedback loop where our nervous system is also regulating theirs. Conversely, when cues of threat and danger imbue nonverbal exchange, nervous system dysregulation tones the relational experience (Porges 1993). Physiologically speaking, then, coregulation is when one nervous system is regulated through connection with another nervous system.

However, this definition of coregulation vastly understates its power and importance, especially when we consider coregulation as a source of anxiety relief. Primarily a felt a sense phenomenon, coregulation emerges in a moment-to-moment relational exchange with another person, moving you out of a solitary experience and into a shared one. Within this shared reality can arise the experience of feeling seen, understood, and validated as well as *feeling felt* (Siegel 2010) by another person. *Feeling felt* can be described as the felt-sense experience of being held within another person's felt-sense experience. Their nonverbal cues, such as the softening of their gaze, shifts in their vocal inflection, and the tilting of their head, communicate that their experience of you resonates within them. When this happens, we come to life because our experiences are validated and made real through another's embodied experience of us.

Feeling felt, as well as feeling seen, known, and validated by another within a relational exchange, highlights the interconnectedness that underpins coregulation. It is this felt awareness of interconnectedness that closes the gap of separation and helps ameliorate feelings of aloneness and anxiety. It creates a felt sense of belonging and of being safely tethered to something greater than our self (Dana 2018). This is the power of coregulation—to experience yourself in a shared reality where you are safe because you are not alone; you are safe because you are not separate.

But if our childhood experiences of coregulation were painful, if our emotional attunement was chronically ruptured in big or little ways, then we do not experience safety in connection, and feelings of aloneness and separateness loom. Further, if early experiences of coregulation were disrupted or unreliable, that compromises our capacity to effectively self-regulate as adults. This is because the ability to self-regulate—the ability to manage emotional fluctuations, thought patterns, and behavioral impulses—emerges from successful coregulating experiences during your young life.

During early developmental years, our little mind-bodies are dependent on our caregivers to create within us a sense of safety and security through a felt sense of togetherness—*You are safe because I am with you; you have nothing to fear because you are not alone.* Over time we internalize those coregulating experiences and they become a part of our internal self-regulating system. In other words, the felt experience of *safety in togetherness* is unconsciously wired into our somatic memory and awakens during times of fear, stress, and distress to help us self-regulate in the absence of opportunities to coregulate (Badenoch 2018). So if our early coregulating experiences were effective, then our ability to self-regulate is enhanced and we possess greater resiliency during times of fear and stress. However, if our early coregulating experiences were inconsistent and chaotic, or compromised by relational lack and unavailability, then we may struggle to effectively settle the fear and anxiety in our nervous system as adults.

To illustrate how ruptures in early coregulating experiences impact your ability to self-regulate as an adult, I will introduce you to my client Cheryl. Cheryl is a kind and sensitive soul who feels very deeply. She places great value on loyalty and makes it a top priority to be there for her friends no matter what. Cheryl regularly puts her own needs aside in order to ensure that her friends are taken care of. She engages in her romantic relationships with the same value system and behavioral proclivities. Despite this, relationships were, in fact, among the primary sources of Cheryl's anxiety.

Specifically, she felt chronic fear and worry about the security of her relationships, both with friends and boyfriends. Further, the degree to which Cheryl depended on her relationships to affirm her sense of self and to help regulate her nervous system was also a source of anxiety. If her relationships didn't feel secure, then Cheryl didn't feel secure. And if this was the case, then she believed it must have been because she did something wrong or because she was "bad" in some way. Because early coregulating experiences can yield an abundance of valuable information about people's sense of self, their relationship patterns, and their ability to manage the fluctuations of their internal world, I promptly began to explore Cheryl's childhood coregulating dynamics.

The youngest of three girls, Cheryl used words like "nuisance," "burden," and "needy" to relate how she often felt in her family. Hypothesizing that these adjectives had something to do with Cheryl's present anxiety in relationships, I probed deeper. I learned that Cheryl had had a close emotional bond with her father, but he had traveled frequently for work and was rarely home. His absence left young Cheryl with a deep sense of longing for connection and a fear that his leaving was really because she was too needy and burdensome. Unfortunately for Cheryl, her mother inadvertently contributed to and reinforced these fears. Overwhelmed by raising three children without much help from her husband, Cheryl's mother wasn't able to tend to Cheryl's emotional needs with much consistency. Further, Cheryl's mother was herself emotionally cold and uncomfortable with displays of affection. It was not uncommon for her mother to chide Cheryl's requests for comfort and reassurance with comments such as, "You're too sensitive," "You need to be stronger," and "I don't like it when you're sad. It makes me uncomfortable." As I learned more about Cheryl's early coregulating experiences, the origins of her anxiety about relationships and her struggle to self-regulate became clearer.

I will return to Cheryl's story in a moment. For now, it is helpful to understand the components of effective coregulation so that you can begin to think about your own coregulating experiences as a child. In doing so, you will glean insight into how those experiences are linked with your anxiety as well as how they influence the degree of comfort and safety you feel in reaching out to others for help in relieving your fear and worry.

Components of Effective Coregulation

Like Cheryl's, no one's early coregulating experience was perfect. Everyone experienced ruptures in their caregiver's attunement to their emotional needs that initiated some kind of adaptive response they carry today. The point is not to judge these imperfections, to minimize their impact, or to pretend they don't exist. The point is to turn toward them and look at them up close to understand how they shaped you and how they contribute to your fear and worry, as well as how they hinder your efforts to effectively mitigate your anxiety through meaningful connection with others.

To identify and understand how early ruptures in coregulating experiences have impacted you, it is helpful to know what a rupture looks like. I will do this by highlighting different components of effective coregulation so that, when you begin to explore your early attachment relationships, the ruptures in coregulation are more noticeable. You will notice that the components are very closely related and even overlap with one another. When integrated, their respective functions combine right and left hemisphere activity to generate a fluid and embodied coregulating experience. The descriptions of the components are followed by exercises that use Mindful

Somatic Awareness to help you move into your implicit world and connect to the sensations that arise when you experience a rupture as it relates to the specific component or components discussed. The visceral sense and subsequent thought processes you have in response to relational ruptures can yield important information about how you may have felt as a child during similar events, as well as how your mind-body coped. With this information, you can begin to identify the obstacles that inhibit you from reaching out and using your present relationships for support, comfort, and reassurance.

Attunement

Attunement is integral to effective coregulation. To experience attunement is to experience the empathic engagement and receptive presence of a nonjudgmental other. When you are attuned to someone else, you are responsive to the verbal *and* nonverbal communications offered in each moment and are thus able to meet the relational needs of the shared experience that support the continuity of connection. During attunement, physiological cues of resonance and safety are exchanged, cues that signal, *I see you, I hear you, I understand you. Keep going. I am here with you.*

With this in mind, it is no wonder that a rupture in coregulation through misattunement can feel so devastating. A break in attunement is often described as feeling *dropped, left,* or *abandoned.* A simple example of misattunement is when you are engaged with another person and they break the connection to look down at their phone. The sudden break in attention, eye contact, and other nonverbal communication is viscerally painful and gives rise to all sorts of emotional, cognitive, and behavioral reactions, especially when the content being shared is important and close to the heart. As an adult, this experience is hurtful. But imagine what this is like as a child, whose experience of the world is a felt one and whose logic is emotionally driven and self-centric (feeling: "I am the cause of the effect").

Exploring Misattunement

Find a quiet place where you will not be disturbed. Take a moment to notice your breath and orient to your body. Once you are more body-aware, recall a time in your life when you experienced a rupture in connection through misattunement. As you recall this moment, SOAR. Once you are fully embodied in the experience, reflect on the thought processes that arise.

As you SOAR through the experience of misattunement, notice the specific sensations that vibrate in response to the disconnect. At what point did you notice the rupture in connection? Was it something that was said or was it a nonverbal cue? If it was nonverbal, what cue caused the rupture? Was it a vocal intonation, a facial gesture, or a particular body movement? What is your somatic response to the rupture? Do you notice any symptoms of your fear response? If so, what are they? What is your behavioral response to the rupture? Do you want to withdraw and move away from the other? Do you want to confront the other? Do you feel frozen? What are the different emotions that come up for you—anger, frustration, shame, guilt, sadness, disappointment, embarrassment, or fear? What thoughts or perceptions do you have about the other as a result of their misattunement? What thoughts or perceptions do you have about yourself? What negative core beliefs arise in response to the rupture? What narratives did you attach to the experience of misattunement?

Now, recall a time when you experienced connection and attunement. As you reflect, SOAR. Answer the same questions listed above. Notice the sensory, emotional, cognitive, and behavioral differences between attunement and misattunement. What might the differences in these experiences tell you about your tendency to turn toward or away from your relationships for comfort? Can you identify any fears of closeness that are linked with experiences of ruptures in coregulation through misattunement?

The intention of this exercise is to help you explore the implicit origins of your present response patterns to ruptures in coregulation through misattunement. This will help you understand your specific fears in reaching out to others for help and how this contributes to your anxiety. Further, it will help you identify ruptures when they happen so you can inhibit a reactive response that might worsen the rupture and, instead, respond through mindful action to help repair the rupture. This exercise, and those that follow, also give you the opportunity to identify and connect to the emotional pain you experienced as a child when you felt emotionally dropped. It enables you to embrace the child within you and compassionately reassure them that they are safe, they are not alone, and they are not at fault.

Understanding and Validation

To feel understood is to feel known, like someone *gets you*. And to feel validated is to feel like someone's understanding of you is *recognized and accepted*. When someone makes an intentional effort to make sense of and validate your perspective, it confirms your sense of self. It also confirms your value as an individual, sending the message that you are worthy of the attention, curiosity, and effort it takes to understand you. Further, it communicates that even if someone expresses a different point of view, yours is still relevant and important. When you feel understood and validated, you have a sense of being connected to something greater, of being part of a collective experience where you are not alone. This is why feeling misunderstood and invalidated can be so devastating. When someone *doesn't* get you or doesn't even *try* to get you, it can feel disconfirming, like an annihilation of you and your reality. This can generate feelings of aloneness, separateness, and shame. For an adult, such an experience can be very upsetting and anxiety provoking, but for a child who, again, does not yet have the emotional and intellectual maturity to make sense of it, the experience can feel incredibly frightening, hurtful, and even despairing.

I Am Because You Know Me

As with the previous exercise, find a quiet place to sit and orient to your body. Once you are more body-aware, recall a time in your life when it was important for you to feel understood and validated but, instead, you felt misunderstood and invalidated. As you recall this moment, SOAR and apply the questions listed in the previous exercise to the experience of feeling misunderstood and invalidated.

Now, recall a time when you felt that someone was genuinely trying to understand and validate your experience. Now SOAR and answer the same questions listed above. Notice the sensory, emotional, cognitive, and behavioral differences between feeling understood and feeling misunderstood. What might the differences in these experiences tell you about your tendency to turn toward or away from your relationships for comfort? What needs for understanding and validation do you have that didn't get met as a child? How might this be part of your anxiety in leaning into your relationships for support?

Empathy and Compassion

Empathy is the ability to imagine yourself in someone else's shoes so you can feel how they might feel. Through empathy, we get as close as possible to feeling what another is feeling. Compassion is a responsiveness to the empathy you experience; it mobilizes empathy into an active effort to alleviate the emotional pain of another. In this way, compassion helps you feel empowered amid the pain and suffering. So you could say that to feel empathy is to *feel felt*, and to feel compassion is to *feel helped*. As with understanding and validation, empathy and compassion touch the interconnectedness that underpins coregulation and helps to ameliorate the felt sense of being alone and powerless in your fear and emotional pain. Further, the experience of empathy and compassion carries the message: *You are important and valuable to me,* a powerful felt sense that can help assuage anxiety and bring peace and calm to your mind-body.

An Empty Heart, a Full Heart

As with the previous exercise, find a quiet place to sit and orient to your body. Now, recall a time in your life when you were in need of empathy and compassion, but your need went unmet. As you recall this moment, SOAR and apply the questions listed in the previous exercise to the experience of feeling alone and without empathy and compassion for your fear and emotional pain.

Now, recall a time when you felt empathy and compassion. As you do this, SOAR and answer the same questions listed above. Notice the sensory, emotional, cognitive, and behavioral differences between feeling someone's emotional presence through empathy and compassion and the absence of their emotional presence. What might the differences in these experiences tell you about your tendency to turn toward or away from your relationships for comfort. What needs for empathy and compassion do you have that didn't get met as a child? How might this dissuade you from seeking comfort in others?

Keep in mind that compassion does not have to be a big gesture. Most often, compassion is experienced in simple things such as a hug or a friend placing their hand on yours during a heartful conversation. Compassion can be an act of kindness, like running an errand for a friend, a phone call during a time of need, or sending an encouraging text. Any effort that demonstrates empathic understanding and a desire to help alleviate emotional pain can be considered compassion.

Coregulation, Rupture, and Repair

Before moving on, it is important to say a few more things about ruptures in coregulation. As discussed, ruptures can be painful and sometimes even harmful. However, they are also inevitable. In fact, it is estimated that during childhood, the back-and-forth reciprocity in coregulation is fluid and without disruption only about a third of the time. The remainder of the time is a series of ruptures with active attempts to repair those ruptures (Schwartz and Maiberger 2018; Dana 2018). In other words, breaches in connection are inevitable, but not irreparable. When coregulation is ruptured, a conscious attempt to empathically reengage and regenerate reciprocity can bring the connection back and support the continuity of the relationship. This tells us that the reparative process is a vital component of effective coregulation and further highlights that ruptures without active repair can be injurious to the relationship and those within it. With this in mind, we can look more closely at how the impact of unrepaired ruptures on a child's mind-body becomes wired into implicit memory and causes anxiety in one's relationships as an adult.

As previously noted, ruptures in coregulation can be emotionally painful for children. Ruptures are often experienced as rejection and precipitate feelings of shame, guilt, and humiliation. When ruptures occur, children may experience themselves as deficient in some way, as if it was some shortcoming within themselves that caused the other to move away from them. Children can also become critical and judgmental of others in an effort to assuage the emotional pain of the rupture and to preserve the integrity of their sense of self (Wilkinson 2010). These experiences then become wired into their implicit body memory and activate during ruptures in coregulation as an adult. This is why you may have strong reactions to simple ruptures in connection now—because old experiences of feeling dropped, shamed, or invalidated are being reexperienced and triggering a defensive response. This also explains, in part, the anxiety you may experience around closeness and intimacy—you anticipate a rupture and all the emotional pain that comes with it, but fear that there will be no opportunity to repair the rupture and bring you back into a place of connection and safety.

However, there is good news. The reparative process can be incredibly healing. When repair is initiated after a rupture and the connection is reestablished, the nervous system moves back into a state of coregulation, back into a shared relational experience. This gives rise to an array of positive feelings of well-being, including joy, excitement, trust, and confidence. With repair, a child learns not to fear a breach in connectedness, because ruptures are temporary. This fosters trust in relationships and attachments to others. Further, with active repair, children experience themselves as important and valuable. They also remain connected to the general goodness of others. They learn to experience others as an integrated whole, with good parts that are pleasing and not-so-good parts that can be disappointing, but who are, overall, worth liking if not loving. And, importantly, the healing power of repair is not exclusive to children. Adults also experience feelings of well-being and a deepened sense of safety in connection when rupture is followed by repair. So when we discuss the harmful effects of ruptures in coregulation, we are also addressing the lack of repair in those ruptures that left the little you feeling bad and overwhelmed and how vestiges of those painful experiences remain wired in your implicit memory and inhibit you from seeking comfort in those you love.

Connect—Disconnect—Reconnect

The following exercise is inspired by the work of Deb Dana (2018) and is intended to help you identify patterns of rupture and repair in your relationships. Cultivating a more intimate understanding of repair or the absence of repair in your relationships can help you identify impediments to finding comfort and reassurance in connectedness with others. This will allow you to heal the emotional wounds that inhibit the reparative process, so you can begin to restore connection when ruptures occur so that closeness feels safe and supportive.

Find a quiet place where you will not be disturbed. Take a moment to notice your breath and orient to your body. Once you are more body-aware, choose a relationship in your life to focus on. As you consider the relationship, SOAR while reflecting on the patterns of reciprocity, rupture, and repair. Notice what it is like when you are experiencing moments of connection. Now, notice what it is like when you experience ruptures in the connection. What sensations do the ruptures activate in your body? What thought patterns, negative core beliefs, or narratives about yourself and the other emerge?

Was there an attempt at repair? If so, who made the attempt? If you did, what did it feel like in your body to reach out and repair? If the other person made the attempt, what was that like to experience? Did you accept the gesture of repair? If so, what did it feel like? If not, why not, and what was the corresponding somatic experience? If there was a repair and the repair was successful, how did your body respond to the reconnection? Did it settle your nervous system and increase feelings of safety and closeness? If the repair was unsuccessful, what sensations, emotions, thoughts, and behaviors did this trigger? Did you experience symptoms of a fear response? What options are available to you to help restore the connection? Now, try this same exercise with another incident or another relationship.

As you notice the patterns of connection and disconnection, pay attention to any parallels they share with how ruptures and repairs were handled in your childhood. Are there any similarities? If so, what are they? Are there any differences? If so, what are they? As you reflect on the similarities and differences, SOAR to try to more intimately understand how your early experiences of repair, or lack thereof, shaped your present response to ruptures and how you still carry remnants of those experiences in your body today.

Let's return to Cheryl to identify how the lack of repair in early coregulating ruptures impacted her felt sense of security in her relationships and contributed to her anxiety. One day in therapy, Cheryl was sharing with me a seemingly minor conflict between two of her friends. Cheryl was, nevertheless, notably distressed about the conflict because she felt compelled to help resolve it but feared her involvement would cause a rift in her relationships with them. As Cheryl was contemplating how to resolve her dilemma, she suddenly paused, looked down, and began to tear up. Concerned, I gently asked Cheryl what was causing her tears. Still looking down, she said, "I feel like you're annoyed with me." As alarming as this was to hear, I nonetheless knew why Cheryl was experiencing me this way—this was what she had experienced (and therefore felt) as a child. Hoping to use this moment to repair early coregulating ruptures, I gently asked Cheryl if there was something I did to cause her this hurt. "No," she said, "you just seem annoyed with me."

I was not the least bit annoyed with Cheryl, but appealing to her logic would have been futile. Cheryl's implicit memory was at the helm and she was experiencing me as her unempathic mother and experiencing herself as being "annoying." My job was to sit with little Cheryl and give her the understanding, validation, empathy, and compassion she longed for as a little girl but rarely received; my job was to help repair the rupture in attunement, so she could experience herself as lovable and our relationship as safe and able to affectionately hold her emotional pain. Facilitating this process in our relationship would help her to experience other relationships as safe, secure, and loving as well.

Because I had been working with Cheryl for some time, she had insight into her early coregulating experiences and how her requests for emotional warmth and comfort were often rejected. And so I softly responded, "I can understand why you might experience me that way. I'm sorry if there was anything I did to cause you this hurt. I would never want to cause you pain." Then, when it felt right, I asked if she was open to challenging her perception of me as annoyed and, instead, imagine that I actually felt deep empathy and compassion for her quandary. She quietly agreed. As soon as she began to shift her perception and allow herself to experience me as a nonjudgmental other who genuinely cared about her emotional hurt, she began to cry.

Cheryl had touched her sadness and her longing to *feel felt;* she had connected to the early unmet need for empathy and compassion she still held in her body. What also surfaced was her fear that any expression of emotional warmth that made her feel securely bonded to someone would be ruptured by her own "neediness" and she would be left feeling rejected, alone, and ashamed. It was the tension between her longing for closeness and fear of rejection that kept Cheryl feeling chronically anxious about the safety and security of her relationships.

When relationships do not feel safe and secure because of chronic ruptures in coregulation, we adapt in the way that best ensures our psychological and emotional survival. Some of us will turn away from relationships and become emotionally self-sufficient. We will disconnect from any felt sense of need for comfort in connection in order to cope with the anxiety that closeness and intimacy trigger. Others of us, like Cheryl, will do the opposite and become dependent on the relationship in an effort to quell the anxiety that connection activates. Both coping styles are attempts to control what feels uncontrollable—the relationship and, therefore, the fear of getting hurt again.

Using Mindful Somatic Awareness as well as the compassionate dynamics of our relationship, Cheryl was able to see that it was her mother's emotional coldness and her father's absence (and not her own neediness) that created the ruptures in her coregulating experience—ruptures that made Cheryl feel like a "burden" and a "nuisance." With this awareness, Cheryl worked to uncouple the sensory, emotional, and cognitive fragments that influenced her perception of herself as "needy" and her perception of relationships as unsafe and insecure. As the over-coupled fragments loosened, she could play with more favorable and accurate ways of seeing and experiencing herself and relationships. She could take risks to authentically show up for her relationships without fear of being too needy and driving people away. And, over time, she was able to disengage from old behavior patterns in which she would endlessly toil to ensure that her relationships were secure. Instead, she began to trust the consistency of her connections and use the warmth and comfort they offered to help relieve her anxiety.

Once again, the somatic lens has shown us how early childhood experiences archive in our implicit memory and influence our perceptions and behavior as adults. Reflecting on our early coregulating experiences enables us to explore the various ways they generate anxiety in closeness and connection with others and therefore inhibit our ability to lean into our adult relationships for the comfort and support we need. Identifying the early ruptures that impair our ability to experience joy and peace in connectivity invites the possibility to heal those ruptures so we can deepen our experience of safety with those we love. And as we will see in the following chapter, when we are able to feel safe and at home with one another and within our own body, we can allow the vulnerability necessary to be fully present, fully alive, and open our hearts to experience the limitless breadth of joy, pleasure, and play in each unfolding moment.

CHAPTER 9

Anxiety and Play

Inherent in the essence of who we are, within the life force energy that gives rise to our experience of being alive, is the magical spark of play. Play is the potential and the ardent desire to unapologetically lose our self in activities that fill our body with joy, excitement, and delight; to be free of the constraints that restrict spontaneous thought and movement; and to engage in activity that reconnects us to the inexhaustible wellspring of creativity and hope that dwells deep within us, uncontaminated by the woe of emotional pain and suffering. Play is a powerful antidote to fear and anxiety, and conversely, fear and anxiety are great inhibitors of play. In this chapter we will explore the various benefits of play and how it fosters the flexibility and resiliency necessary to adapt to the ever-changing world around you and within you. We will also use the somatic lens to illuminate the various ways early childhood experiences and dynamics inhibit your ability to play as an adult, so you can begin to heal the pain that dampens your capacity for pleasure and delight. Overarchingly, the intention of this chapter is to encourage appreciation and reverence for the wonder of play and to help you make it a natural and normal aspect of your daily life so that you can quell the anxiety that inhibits your ability to live freely, authentically, and with an open heart.

Play takes many forms; it is as varied as the day. What constitutes play for one person can seem like misery to another. But no matter what form it takes, the notion of play implies fun, self-enjoyment, a felt sense of flow, and freedom from time and thought restraints. It even implies imagination, mystery, and enchantment—the discovery of new sensations, ideas, and ways of seeing and engaging the world around you. Importantly, though, the notion of play also implies a sense of safety and security. To be open to the spontaneity inherent in play and the unpredictability that comes with it, your mind-body must feel safe to expand and welcome the unknown. But as we have learned, if remnants of unresolved fears remain woven throughout your implicit memory system, the very idea of uninhibited receptivity and responsiveness to the present moment can be anxiety inducing. If it is, play is not pleasurable, and it is therefore not able to uplift your life and help sustain a felt sense of hope and optimism in times of fear and stress.

Play and the Autonomic Nervous System

Play requires a unique collaboration of both the sympathetic nervous system (SNS) and the parasympathetic nervous system (PNS) to regulate swift changes in energy flow. Much like a seesaw, energy arousal during play naturally rises and falls as physical movement, blood flow, heart rate, and breathing fluctuate. Remember, the SNS is responsible for galvanizing energy supply to mobilize the body for action, and this includes play activities. The PNS downregulates energy arousal, facilitating calm, rest, and restoration, which is also required of many play activities. And as we have just learned, the PNS also enables social engagement and connection with others, which can be an integral part of certain types of play. As you can see, in any given moment, depending on the activity, play draws on each of these special attributes of the autonomic nervous system. Smooth transitions between excitation, calmness, and social engagement are made possible through the cooperative efforts of the SNS and PNS to regulate the ebb and flow of energy inherent in play (Dana 2018).

When we look at the dynamic interplay between the SNS and PNS during play, we can begin to see and appreciate how play fosters the flexibility and resiliency necessary for your nervous system to successfully adapt to the ongoing changes in the world around you and within you. Play requires a unique alternation of high and low arousal states. Play is also fun and pleasurable. When varying body states of excitation are coupled with positive experiences, as is the case with play, the nervous system learns to swiftly adapt to changing environmental demands while also holding onto the same felt sense of hope and optimism intrinsic in play. In this way, play strengthens the nervous system's ability to regulate its responsiveness to stimulation, and augments its flexibility and adaptation to a broad array of life events and circumstances (Ogden and Fisher 2015). It also enhances the resiliency of the nervous system so it can rebound from stress and adversity more quickly and completely.

Engaging in the wonder and delight of play also enhances collaboration of right and left hemisphere functioning. Play is the fountainhead of imagination, creativity, sensation, new ideas, and new perspectives—right and left hemisphere phenomena that allow us to fully attune to our intuitive knowing and present-moment awareness *and* to look ahead to the future to *play* with possible scenarios and ideas and analyze their outcomes. The cooperation of right and left hemisphere functioning through play enhances existing neural connections, creates new ones, and links various brain centers to augment overall functioning (Brown 2009). As neural connections are strengthened and the brain centers collaborate more efficiently and effectively, we are able to transfer what we learn in play into a variety of contexts in our lives, allowing us to adapt and thrive in a wide range of different environments.

When we are equipped with a robust and flexible nervous system, able to roll with the ups and downs of life, and when our right and left hemispheres are reliably integrated, able to think, feel, and intuit, we feel capable, empowered, and safe to welcome the uncertainty in each unfolding moment. And we feel hopeful or even excited for the opportunity to rise to any challenge we are faced with and to test our innate grit and prowess. This is the tremendous value of play—to foster flexibility, resiliency, joy, and hope; to cultivate internal resources that regulate fear, reduce anxiety, and foster excitement in possibility.

Reconnecting to Play and Playfulness

The following is a simple exercise intended to acquaint you with the activities that ignite the spark of play within you. As noted above, anxiety clamps the ability to play. Add to this the fast-paced hullabaloo of everyday living and you have a recipe for a life bereft of pleasure and play. Over time this results in a disconnect and even a forgetting of what particular brand of *joie de vivre* delights your heart and lifts your spirit. The following is a list of activities to help you remember the type of play you are drawn to or that you might like to include in your life. On a separate piece of paper, list the activities that resonate with you. This list is not exhaustive, so if there is a play activity you enjoy doing but that is not listed here, write it down.

Activities of Play and Playfulness:

Arts and crafts (such as coloring, drawing, painting, sculpting, or knitting)

Playing board games, cards, charades, or other indoor games

Assembling a puzzle

Reading

Singing or playing an instrument

Dancing

Playing a sports game (such as catch, hoops, Frisbee, or tag)

Bike riding

Swimming and doing cannonball jumps

Running through sprinklers

Water fights (with water balloons, hose)

Playing fetch with your dog

Playing in the rain or snow

Swinging on a swing set

Skipping rocks over water

Building a sandcastle

Counting stars at night or finding shapes in the clouds

Hanging out with friends, sharing stories, telling jokes, and laughing out loud

Baking, cooking, or enjoying new culinary fare

Eating favorite ice cream or candy

Remember, play can range from high-intensity activities to low-intensity activities. The key markers of play are: pleasure, freedom from time and self-consciousness, potential for creativity and spontaneity, being voluntary, and being intrinsically desirable (done for its own sake)—you do it because you want to (Brown 2009). So long as the activities you are drawn to reflect these qualities in some way, then they likely are play activities.

  Next, find a quiet place where you will not be disturbed. Bring your attention to your breath and then to the rest of your body. Once you are more body-aware, refer to your list of play activities. One at a time, go through the list and imagine yourself engaging in each play activity. As you do this, SOAR. How does your body respond? Do you experience positive sensations? If so, what are they? Does your body experience unpleasant sensations? If so, articulate them aloud. As you imagine yourself engaging in the activity, make a conscious plan to do it in the near future. As you make this plan, how does your body respond? What thoughts arise? Is your mind-body finding reasons not to do the activity? Is your body-mind determined to do the activity, no matter what? Are you vacillating between making it happen and letting it go? Notice your mind-body process around incorporating play into your life: this will help you identify the obstacles that prevent you from engaging in pleasurable activities.

  So far, we have highlighted the value and importance of play. But what happens when fun and playful activities are missing from your life? To help demonstrate how anxiety can precipitate the absence of play and how a deficit in joyful activities perpetuates anxiety, I will introduce you to my client Sam. An earnest man with a formidable stature and plodding gait, Sam came to me at the urging of his wife, who had grown increasingly frustrated with his endless work schedule. She wanted Sam to get help so he could understand his resistance to taking time off and relaxing.

  Sam was a successful entrepreneur and an "all work and no play" kind of guy. In any given moment, he had a dozen irons in the fire and was always looking to add another. His busy work schedule kept him in constant motion and precluded any opportunity to engage in fun and playful activities. Needless to say, there was little time to devote to his marriage, which was beginning to show signs of neglect. Though work was important to Sam, so was his marriage, and he was committed to reducing his workload so he could spend more time with his wife, take vacations, and enjoy the fruits of his labor. He just didn't know how. Every time Sam tried to work less and enjoy free time, he felt "lazy" and "useless," with a sense of "urgency" as if he was missing a rare, singular opportunity for more work. The symptoms Sam experienced when he tried to work less and engage in playful activities reflected anxiety, which made me think that work was a way Sam managed his worry and stress and coped with old, unresolved fears.

Curious about his childhood and how it helped shape a mindset so hyperfocused on work and so critical of pleasure and play, I inquired about Sam's young life. He shared with me that he grew up in a home that valued hard work and achievement. His father, in particular, was a well-educated man with several degrees *and* several businesses. Though now in his eighties, his father still worked seven days a week, from sunup to sundown. As a boy, whenever Sam would respond to his natural instincts to ride a bike or read comic books, his father would censure him and remind him that hard work doesn't include frivolous interests. One time in particular, Sam recalled going outside to do yard work, one of his many weekend chores. Between raking the leaves and mowing the lawn, Sam decided to climb the giant pepper tree in their backyard; he wanted to see if he could reach the highest branch. As he scaled the tree, he suddenly heard his father yell from the back porch, "The lawn won't mow itself." Crestfallen, Sam began his descent and resumed his chores.

Inhibitors of Play

Though not everyone can relate to the specific dynamics of Sam's young life, many of us can relate to certain aspects of the way his early environment inhibited fun and spontaneity, specifically the deficit in a felt sense of safety and freedom to engage in play. When the emotional tone of the home during childhood is stern and strict, or volatile and unpredictable, it inhibits feelings of safety. And as we now know, a felt sense of safety is imperative to allow the vulnerability necessary to be fully present, fully open, and fully alive. In this way, safety is a prerequisite of play. If this prerequisite is not met, it becomes difficult to surrender to the joy and pleasure intrinsic in play. Sam's story demonstrates this well. It also demonstrates how negative emotions, thought patterns, and core beliefs can become over-coupled with play when pleasure-seeking instincts are not met with approval and encouragement.

As an adult, whenever Sam tried to take time off and do something fun, he felt "lazy," "useless," and anxious about work. These thoughts and feelings reflected the somatic remnants of the implicit messages his father had communicated through his reactions to Sam's play, as well as the modeling of his own unrelenting work schedule. The negative thoughts and feelings Sam now coupled with play reflected the substantial power of the early environment to influence conscious and unconscious attitudes toward leisure and pleasure. If the primary people in a child's life do not welcome the energy of lightheartedness and play, but instead attach to it negative value judgments and regard it as wasteful, inappropriate, or even disrespectful, the message sent to the child is that play is in some way not okay. Sadly, when this happens, the instinct to play, which is a felt-sense phenomenon, becomes coupled with negative thoughts and feelings. Play is then imbued with anxiety and becomes something to be avoided, or to be engaged in only rarely and cautiously.

Though one might understand, accept, and believe in the value of play, if childhood experiences of play are dampened by a strict, disapproving, or volatile parent, or if a high premium is placed on performance and free time is considered wasteful, then the ability to be relaxed and unselfconscious is diminished and the spark of play can be extinguished. With this in mind, it is important to consider the emotional tone of play during your formative years. If your family dynamics restricted positive feelings, spontaneous movement, and the laughter, squeals, and other joyful noises that accompany play, then the origins of your struggle to give way to pleasure-seeking activities are linked, in part, to these early experiences.

Play and Coregulation

Cultivating the capacity to play requires safe and secure coregulating experiences. If early attachment relationships felt reliable, reassuring, and accepting of your authentic self-expression, then the mind-body feels free to yield to whims of joy and delight. Positive coregulating experiences support the flexibility and resiliency of the autonomic nervous system because they lovingly create space for the entire range of emotions to be experienced, from positive to negative, without judgment or censure. This is necessary to foster the integrity of the nervous system to handle all aspects of life, including play. For example, when a child is playing catch and misses the ball, an attuned parent will validate and empathize with the disappointment and frustration the child is experiencing while encouraging the child to try again. Illustrated in this example is the child's experience of pleasure (in trying to catch the ball), disappointment (in missing the ball), and hope (in trying to catch the ball again). Smooth and supported transitions up and down the spectrum of emotions foster the flexibility and resiliency your nervous system needs to manage the ever-changing demands of the environment around you and your relationships within it. They also foster a sense of optimism and empowerment in knowing that unpleasant feelings don't last forever and that the ability to recover from them is possible and self-possessed; that is, the power to recover is within you.

But what happens if play is met with negative coregulating experiences? For example, imagine this same child trying to catch the ball and then missing the ball. Instead of receiving the encouragement needed to try again, she receives from her parents a disapproving glare or plain indifference. In this situation, the child's experience of play, which includes the risk she took to succeed in catching the ball, is left with a coupling of play with failure and disapproval. Experiences such as this, especially when they are chronic or emotionally intense, restrict the adaptability of the nervous system and its ability to rebound from adversity. Further, they imbue the experience of play with anxiety, and even drudgery and pessimism.

Anxiety and Quiet Play

Sometimes pleasure and play are quiet and leisurely, requiring only enough effort to turn a page if you are reading or to stir a pot if you are cooking. Nonetheless, anxiety can also thwart these attempts at play, making it difficult to quiet your mind-body. The ability to be still and savor simple, quiet pleasures requires activation of the PNS, the branch of the autonomic nervous system responsible for rest, relaxation, and restoration. However, as you may remember, the PNS is also responsible for the *freeze* defense response. If you struggle with quiet play, this is relevant to know because the unresolved fear at the core of your anxiety may include the experience of freezing (or immobilization) in the face of danger or stress.

If your anxiety is linked to a frightening, highly stressful, or overwhelming experience during which you were not able to mobilize the response necessary to make you feel safe and protected, then this may explain why relaxing your body in quiet play can be difficult for you. As previously noted, fear and stress can lead to immobilization or freezing if you are not able to engage an effective defense response (fight or flight). And as we now know, the freeze response is initiated by acute PNS activation. Well, what happens when you engage in quiet play? Your PNS is activated, initiating a physiological state very close to immobilization. So, if inscribed in your implicit memory system are experiences of immobility when confronted with threat or danger, then relaxing your body can be a very difficult thing to do. Why? Because the physical sensation of relaxing your body and being still has become over-coupled with the sensation of fear, powerlessness, and other intense negative emotions (Levine 2010). Additionally, relaxing your body has the potential to release or *thaw* the underlying fear that remains frozen (or immobilized) in your nervous system. The discharge of this fear can flood the body with intense emotions and distress. Also, mind-body states of calmness interfere with mobility and hypervigilance. If unresolved fears (related to thwarted efforts to protect yourself) are frozen in your nervous system, then your mind-body believes that it must at all times remain hypervigilant and ready to marshal defensive action. Relaxing your body interferes with these efforts and increases a sense of threat and danger, which can lead to an increased connection to negative emotions and body sensations (Ogden and Fisher 2015).

So if immobilization or freezing is a part of your historical fear-based experience, then when you engage in quiet play, your body may try to resist it. In these instances, your body will not allow you to relax and loosen your muscular constriction, because to do so does not feel safe. Instead, your body will try to stay mobilized and vigilant, because so long as you are in motion, you will not be in danger.

Reflecting on Play

The aim of this exercise is to reflect on memories of play, so you can begin to identify the sensations, emotions, and core beliefs you associate with play activities. In acquainting yourself with your mind-body reaction to play, you can begin to recognize inhibitors of play and explore their origins.

Find a quiet place free from distraction. Take a moment to notice your breath and orient to your body. Once you are more body-aware, recall a play activity you used to do as a child. As you recall this moment, SOAR: sense, observe, articulate, and reflect. As you SOAR through the embodied memory of play, notice the specific sensations that arise in your body. Are they pleasurable? Does your body relax and welcome the sensation? Or do you feel currents of anxiety? Does your body restrict in response to pleasurable and relaxing sensations? What are the different emotions that arise—joy, excitement, hopeful anticipation, or delight? Or frustration, shame, guilt, embarrassment, or anxiety? What thoughts or perceptions do you have about play and about yourself as you play? What core beliefs arise in response to remembering play as a child? What narratives come up as you recall this play memory? How do the thoughts and feelings you are experiencing inhibit your present attitude toward play and the degree to which you incorporate it into your life?

Now that we know a little bit more about anxiety and play, let's return to Sam. We know that Sam's early experiences of play were largely shut down by his father, who devalued fun and games, believing them to be a frivolous pastime. With this came all sorts of negative thoughts and feelings about play that impacted Sam's ability to enjoy recreation and leisure. But through Mindful Somatic Awareness, Sam discovered an inhibitor to play of which he had not been fully conscious.

One day in session, Sam was sharing with me pressures he was experiencing at work with regard to an associate. Specifically, his work associate, who was an avid surfer, was going to Australia to catch some waves at one of the world's top surf meccas. His leaving was putting a kink in Sam's work agenda, which was causing strain around some deadlines. Wanting to explore his anxiety around play, I asked, "Have you ever been to Australia?" "No," Sam replied, "though it looks beautiful. The surf is great." A bit confused, I asked, "Oh. Do you surf?" "No," Sam responded, "but I've always wanted to." Sam proceeded to speak somewhat poetically about what he imagined it would be like to "ride a wave" and how "peaceful" it would be "out on the water." So I asked Sam why he didn't try surfing. "What would my wife think?" he replied. That one caught me off guard. It caught Sam by surprise, too, who looked at me with shock and said, "Well, I wasn't expecting that."

It turned out that Sam feared his wife would judge him if he were to take up surfing, or any play activity for that matter. The irony was not lost on Sam, since it was his wife who was constantly pressing him to incorporate fun and play into his life. On the surface, this made sense—Sam's father was critical of play, so why wouldn't he perceive his wife to be the same way? What made it so surprising was the degree to which Sam didn't see it. That is, he had no idea that he perceived his wife this way. It wasn't until he spontaneously said it out loud that he became conscious of it. And as he explored this fear, he realized that he feared judgment not only from his wife, but from everyone whose opinions of him he cared about. It was very important to Sam's identity and sense of self that he be regarded as a hardworking, successful businessman. He felt that if he engaged in play, it would mar this image and he would lose the respect of his wife and work associates.

Through Mindful Somatic Awareness, Sam probed his implicit, sensory world that held this fear—a fear that stemmed in part from unhealed emotional wounds from his father's harsh judgment of Sam's playful impulses. Over time, as he connected to his somatic self, he began to challenge his fear that he would be criticized and seen as indolent if he engaged in pleasurable activities. And as he challenged these fears, he was slowly able to work through his belief that he would lose the respect of his wife and colleagues if he took time off to enjoy activities that fed his interests and playful impulses. Each weekend, Sam decided to do something fun, however small, that would allow him to enjoy the fruits of all his hard work. And the more Sam engaged in play activities, the more the criticism and backlash he once believed were inevitable consequences of pastimes gradually uncoupled from his fear, creating room for a new way of seeing and experiencing fun. Eventually Sam took a big leap and took that vacation to Australia. There, under the warm Australian sun, in the beautiful ocean water, Sam took surf lessons and learned to ride the waves.

Everyday Play

The purpose of this exercise is to broaden your awareness of fleeting moments of joy and playfulness in your everyday life. Whether it is a direct experience you have or something you notice in others, take note of the countless ways fun and laughter pop up in each unfolding moment.

Each day over the next week, do your best to be aware of playful and fun moments that you initiate or that others initiate. Also pay attention to when others are enjoying themselves and having fun. At the end of each day, write them down in a journal. Within a week, you will be able to see just how many instances of play or opportunities for fun were present in your life. If you struggle to notice moments of play, make it a goal to list at least two instances a day. Sometimes it can be overwhelming to start new behaviors, so setting realistic expectations can help make the exercises less daunting and increase your chances of sticking with it.

Remember that play comes in all shapes and sizes. To help you identify moments of fun or play or joy, the following is a list of categories to help you.

Spontaneous actions

Deliberate activities of fun and pleasure

Jokes and puns

Finding humor in things that happen or random moments

Laughing or simply smiling

Being silly

A life without play is a life unable to expand and experience its full potential. Play is truly unique in its ability to enrich our felt sense of being alive. How cool is it that our emotional health is enhanced by simply engaging in activities of self-enjoyment! And how tragic it is that the ability to enjoy ourselves and enhance our authentic experience of life and living can be so sorely hindered by old, unresolved fears. Once again, however, the somatic lens shows us that the old wounds that keep us stuck in fear and dampen the spark of play within us can be healed. By turning inward to feel the somatic resonance of painful childhood experiences, you can access the innate wisdom of the body that can guide you toward healing those wounds that inhibit your impulse to play. And as the fear and emotional pain slowly fade, your innate impulse to experience joy and delight will expand and you can begin to live in reverence and wonder of the amazing life force that you are.

CHAPTER 10

Anxiety and the Healing Journey

The decision to work through old unresolved fears to relieve your anxiety is really a decision to evolve and transform. It is a decision to turn inward to examine your inner life and heal the deep emotional wounds that hinder the organic unfolding of your authentic self. From this place of honest reflection and vulnerability emerges insight and understanding that release you from fear and guide you in the direction of your highest, truest self. The mindset needed to facilitate your evolution of Self is one that embraces what I believe is a dynamic paradox at the core of the healing journey, that is: Healing enables the organic unfolding of your authentic self *and,* at the very same time, it *is* the organic unfolding of your authentic self. Healing is the co-arising of *what is* (you as you are) and *what can be* (the you that you can become). Just like the oak tree contained within the acorn, your highest Self is contained within you. The decision to heal sets the intention to become your greatest self and releases the energetic potential to facilitate that becoming. *And,* at the very same time you are becoming your potential, in each and every moment you are perfect and exactly where you need to be. To know and accept this paradox, that you are both perfect and perfection becoming, creates a mindset that infuses the healing journey with a sense of hope and trust that all is well and as it should be, a reassurance that is sorely needed during what can often feel like a forbidding and uncertain process. Embracing the dynamic paradox at the heart of the healing journey helps facilitate a rich transformative process and keeps you afloat when the weight of the inner work feels too heavy to keep going.

In addition to embracing this paradox, it is helpful to know and embrace a few intrinsic principles of the healing process itself. This will give you a better sense of what to expect throughout your journey and provide reassurance when the road feels confusing and uncertain. So often in my practice my clients are making real and important progress in their work, but they don't always see it or believe it, even when I reflect it back to them. This is because they approach the process with a very specific idea of what they want their healing to look like or think it should look like. When this doesn't happen, they get stuck in trying to force their process to happen in a certain way. While this is a natural symptom of transformation (one that you can expect despite this warning), you can mitigate its impact by accepting a few inherent principles of the healing journey. Let's begin with the very nature and purpose of fear.

Fear is an emotion rich in wisdom and it will not go away—it's not designed to. Remember, fear is not the problem, it is your response to fear that is causing your anxiety. The goal is to regulate your fear response, not to get rid of fear. When your fear response integrates right and left hemisphere functioning, then your ability to see, think, and feel are clearer. This allows fear to serve its inherent function—to provide information to help you navigate your life. When fear is no longer feared, it becomes a useful emotion. Like all the other emotions, fear intends to help us make important decisions. It asks us to pause and reflect on what is happening and consider how to best proceed. Fear helps guide us away from that which can harm us or that which does not align with our greatest good and it points us toward what feels right and true. In this way, fear actually helps us create a life of purpose and authenticity. When you accept the intrinsic value of fear, your expectations of what anxiety relief actually looks and feels like will change, and you will shift your focus from trying to get rid of your fear to understanding it and using it to guide your present-moment experience. Herein, relief from anxiety naturally arises.

The road to healing old unresolved fears necessitates that you change how you see fear. However, it also necessitates that you change how you see yourself. So another principle of the healing journey is that you engage your process with complete honesty. One of the hardest things to do is to let go of your narratives and to see yourself, your loved ones, and your lived experiences as they really are, not as you want them to be. There is great safety in the stories you tell yourself, even though these very stories perpetuate your anxiety. Honesty requires a willingness to challenge these narratives and the thoughts and feelings contained within them, so you can know the truth of your subjective experience. And as this truth emerges and you are able to work through and release the emotional energy bound up with these early wounding experiences, there is a corresponding reparative process that brings your mind-body back into alignment with its instinctive drive to become its potential.

Beware, however, of your resistance to honesty—it's sneaky. Though it is generally undisputed that honesty is imperative for a fruitful healing journey, it nonetheless triggers resistance when it comes up against a commonly held belief—the belief that in looking at difficult, painful, or not so pleasant aspects of yourself, others, and your experiences, you are dwelling on the negative or lingering in the past. And that in doing so, you are hindering the healing endeavor and keeping yourself from moving beyond your fear and worry. I understand and have great compassion for this plea. But if you're concerned that the reflective process will mire you in the past and in negative energy, keep in mind what you now know about implicit memory. For the anxious person, unresolved frightening and overwhelming experiences of the past are repeatedly showing up in the present. To deny this will keep you stuck in the past and in the negative emotions linked with it. But to look at your past with open and honest eyes is to give yourself the opportunity to understand these historical experiences, so you can identify them when they reappear in the present. When you can see the past in the present, you are given the choice to reengage in old patterns *or* to move beyond them and create new and healthy ones. This is how you move beyond the painful wounds of your past and raise the vibrational quality of your present-moment experience.

Another obstacle that hinders honest reflection is the tendency to think that you are complaining when you articulate the hurt you feel from past wounds. This may be because you think that no matter how painful the old wounds you carry are, others have it worse. Or because those who hurt you did not mean to and they did the best they could. Or because you probably did something to deserve it. Again, I have great compassion for these pleas and understand them intimately. But I encourage you to peel back the layers of these responses to examine their origins and consider how they help protect you from the vulnerability inherent in emotional exploration. I would also encourage you to challenge and SOAR through them to see what healing exists for you beyond them.

To reflect on your emotional pain is not an exercise in self-pity, ingratitude, or blame—not unless that is your conscious intention. Rather, it is an exercise that honors your life, which includes your emotional pain and suffering. Your soul needs to feel seen and known and to be treated with respect, just as much as your body needs food and water. When such nourishment is withheld, or provided conditionally or inconsistently, it gravely impacts your health and well-being. It threatens your sense of safety in the world and can cause you to question your sense of value and purpose. To explore the rich nuances of your inner world and the unresolved pains contained therein creates an opportunity to validate what you endured and the struggle it took to endure it. These are sacred life events that shaped you and they deserve recognition. From this place you can begin to release the energy of your emotional injuries and heal your suffering. And when your heart is free from suffering, a deep connection to your inherent purpose and self-worth emerges, which naturally engenders an effortless gratitude for the blessing of life and the blessings in your life.

All this talk about honesty is easier said than done, which is why the healing journey also requires a courageous heart. To be honest is to be willing to see things clearly and truthfully; to be courageous is to accept and put into practice what your honesty reveals to you. There is great risk when you choose to accept the truth of your lived experiences and integrate this new reality into the way you see and engage with the world. Your attempts to change may often be met with resistance from those around you who do not understand your new perspective or who do not like the way your new choices impact them. To make these changes, you risk feeling misunderstood and invalidated when you are not seen the way you want or intend to be. You also risk not being liked and accepted by those you love and need. Or you risk moments of confrontation when your actions have upset others. As a child, you adapted to your environment to ensure that your needs were met and that you would be okay. These adaptations follow you into adulthood and can feel just as vital to your survival now as they did when you were young. To actively challenge old perceptions and to change what has felt like the most effective way to survive requires immeasurable courage.

In my practice, my clients will often invalidate or minimize their efforts to change because their attempts at doing so didn't go exactly the way they envisioned or their efforts did not yield the results they wanted. They then tend to scold themselves for not having been stronger, quicker, calmer, or whatever they intended to be. Sadly, when their focus is on chiding themselves for the outcome of their efforts, they overlook the immense courage it took to enact the change in the first place. Further, they are distracted from noticing the small and subtle changes that did take place—changes that, over time, create the overarching change they desire.

There is immeasurable value in setting an intention and following through with that intention, no matter the outcome. This is where change begins, and it takes great courage to initiate these steps. So on your healing journey, remember to honor the courage it takes to enact change. Do not underestimate the valor inherent in your efforts. During moments of frustration, confusion, and uncertainty, remember that you are exactly where you need to be *and* that to have reached this destination means you have demonstrated the courage necessary to get there. If you find you are focusing on what you didn't do or what didn't happen, pause and SOAR, and then notice at least one aspect of the process that is different from before. In doing so, you will improve your ability to see the subtle shifts that are taking place. Over time, you will notice that the cumulative effect of these subtle shifts is the very change you have been working so hard to achieve.

To faithfully hold onto the healing mindset and engage your process of transformation with honesty and courage, you must surrender to the healing process. This is why surrender is among the essential principles of the healing journey. The road to healing is long and winding, full of unexpected twists and turns that lead you through places of darkness, confusion, and uncertainty as well as through places of light, clarity, and awe. Sometimes you feel confident that you are headed in the right direction, while at other times you feel certain you took a wrong turn somewhere. Sometimes the destination appears very clear, while other times you wonder where in the world you are headed. Because the healing process feels so unpredictable, there is often an earnest and determined effort to control it. That is understandable. But the direction of your healing path is not determined by your conscious mind; it is determined by the wisdom of the life force within you that knows exactly where you need to go *and* how to get there. So the healing journey requires a daily practice of surrender. Each and every day you must seek to release your efforts to coerce the unfolding of your process in the direction of what you want or think you need.

It is very easy to become attached to an idea of what your healing journey should look like or what outcome is most beneficial for you. Your tendency to do this is innate: it is a natural function of the left hemisphere—to analyze the present situation and make determinations based on what you logically deduce. Because you are designed to think this way, it is very difficult to resist using your logic to determine the direction of your healing. But to rely solely on your left hemisphere to guide your process denies the intelligence of your right hemisphere and its powerful connection to the wisdom of your body. The job of the left hemisphere is to execute the guidance offered by the intuitive, somatic knowing of the right hemisphere. To surrender to intuitive knowing and allow your right hemisphere to lead can be incredibly unnerving, because the knowing offered by your somatic self isn't always obvious and doesn't always feel certain. It requires faith both in the wisdom of your body and in your attunement to the somatic vibrations that carry that wisdom.

With this in mind, it is very important to remember how difficult it is to surrender, and to have compassion for yourself when you slide back into old efforts to control the trajectory and outcome of your healing. Like a muscle that can be strengthened only through daily exercise, your ability to surrender will improve through daily practice. When you set the intention to surrender and you practice your intention daily, you will gradually improve your ability to release your attachment to your ideas of what your transformation should look like and trust the wisdom of your body to guide it in the direction of your highest Self.

There is one last essential principle of the healing journey that is critical to mention—the principle of endurance. The healing journey necessitates endurance: the ability to carry on despite the fatigue and doubt that can threaten to deter your efforts. Though there are moments of beauty, light, and grace amid your process of transformation, there are also moments of darkness, weariness, and confusion. The honesty and courage needed to power your healing journey and keep it in motion require effort that regularly drains your energy. Additionally, the ongoing practice of surrender can be fatiguing, particularly when circumstances feel markedly unsteady and unstable. The pull to revert to old behavior patterns that are familiar and predictable can be exceedingly strong, and also unconscious. Constant energy is needed to resist powerful desires to control and to remain vigilant of subtle tendencies to reengage in old ways of doing. Endurance is needed to keep moving forward despite how questionable the whole process feels. Patience is also needed.

Inherent in the quality of endurance is patience—the ability to accept delay in the fulfillment of your longing to experience relief from your chronic fear and worry. To contain your restlessness during the time it takes to achieve deep and lasting change and to persevere despite your frustration with the process are very important. This isn't to say that you will not experience noticeable and notable relief along the way; it is simply to say that to integrate the changes you make into your general way of doing things takes time. But rest assured, with patience and endurance, the intention of your efforts to heal your emotional wounds will manifest as the change you are seeking to create.

Throughout your healing journey, there will be times when your perceptions will tell you that your efforts are futile, and you will want to give up. But if you accept the key principles of the healing journey and hold onto the dynamic paradox at the heart of your transformation, you will know that the fatigue and doubt you feel are merely symptoms of the process and not indicators of the outcome. Always remember, you are perfect *and* you are perfection becoming; you are exactly where you need to be and you already possess everything you need to become your highest Self. If you can hold onto this truth, then when you feel tired and weary, you will not give up. Rather, with loving compassion, you will simply allow yourself to rest.

References

Badenoch, B. 2018. *The Heart of Trauma: Healing the Embodied Brain in the Context of Relationships*. New York: W. W. Norton and Company.

Brown, S. 2009. *Play: How It Shapes the Brain, Opens the Imagination, and Invigorates the Soul*. New York: Penguin.

Damasio, A., H. Damasio, and D. Tranel. 2012. "Persistence of Feelings and Sentience After Bilateral Damage of the Insula." *Cerebral Cortex* 23(4): 833-846.

Dana, D. 2018. *The Polyvagal Theory in Therapy: Engaging the Rhythm of Regulation*. New York: W. W. Norton and Company.

Gendlin, E. T. 1978. *Focusing*. New York: Bantam Books.

Levine, P. 2005. *Healing Trauma: A Pioneering Program for Restoring the Wisdom of Your Body*. Boulder, CO. Sounds True.

Levine, P. 2010. *In an Unspoken Voice: How the Body Releases Trauma and Restores Goodness*. Berkeley, CA: North Atlantic Books.

Levine, P., R. Selvam, and L. A. Parker. 2003. "Somatic Experiencing: Coupling Dynamics." *Somatic Experiencing Training Module Two*. Available at www.psyche-koerper.de/pdfs/artikel_coupling_dynamics.pdf

Namkung, H., S. H. Kim, and A. Sawa. 2017. "The Insula: An Underestimated Brain Area in Clinical Neuroscience, Psychiatry, and Neurology." *Trends in Neuroscience* 40(4): 200-207.

Ogden, P., and J. Fisher. 2015. *Sensorimotor Psychotherapy: Interventions for Trauma and Attachment.* New York: W. W. Norton and Company.

Payne, P., P. Levine, and M. Crane-Godreau. 2015. "Somatic Experiencing: Using Interoception and Proprioception as Core Elements of Trauma Therapy." *Frontiers in Psychology* 6:93: 1-18.

Porges, S. 1993. "The Infant's Sixth Sense: Awareness and Regulation of Bodily Processes." *Zero to Three: Bulletin of the National Center for Clinical Infant Programs* 14: 12-16.

Porges, S. 2011. *The Polyvagal Theory: Neurobiological Foundation of Emotions, Attachment, Communication, and Self-Regulation.* New York: W. W. Norton and Company.

Rothschild, B. 2000. *The Body Remembers: The Psychophysiology of Trauma and Trauma Treatment.* New York: W. W. Norton and Company.

Schwartz, A., and Maiberger, B. 2018. *EMDR Therapy and Somatic Psychology: Interventions to Enhance Embodiment in Trauma Treatment.* New York: W. W. Norton and Company.

Siegel, D. J. 2010. *Mindsight: The New Science of Personal Transformation.* New York: Bantam Books.

Siegel, D. J. 2013. *Brainstorm: The Power and Purpose of the Teenage Brain.* New York: Jeremy P. Tarcher/Penguin.

Wilkinson, M. 2010. *Changing Minds in Therapy: Emotion, Attachment, Trauma, and Neurobiology.* New York: W. W. Norton and Company.

Michele L. Blume, PsyD, SEP, is a licensed clinical psychologist, somatic experiencing practitioner (SEP), and certified Reiki practitioner. She is also trained in eye movement desensitization and reprocessing (EMDR) therapy. Her work focuses on mind-body integration to heal developmental trauma. Blume works in private practice in Redondo Beach, CA. To learn more about her, visit www.dr micheleblume.com.

Foreword writer **Arielle Schwartz, PhD**, is a licensed clinical psychologist, EMDR therapy consultant, and certified yoga instructor with a private practice in Boulder, CO. She is author of *The Complex PTSD Workbook* and *The Post-Traumatic Growth Guidebook*, and coauthor of *EMDR Therapy and Somatic Psychology*.

Real change *is* possible

For more than forty-five years, New Harbinger has published proven-effective self-help books and pioneering workbooks to help readers of all ages and backgrounds improve mental health and well-being, and achieve lasting personal growth. In addition, our spirituality books offer profound guidance for deepening awareness and cultivating healing, self-discovery, and fulfillment.

Founded by psychologist Matthew McKay and Patrick Fanning, New Harbinger is proud to be an independent, employee-owned company. Our books reflect our core values of integrity, innovation, commitment, sustainability, compassion, and trust. Written by leaders in the field and recommended by therapists worldwide, New Harbinger books are practical, accessible, and provide real tools for real change.

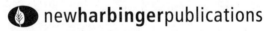 **newharbinger**publications

MORE BOOKS from
NEW HARBINGER PUBLICATIONS

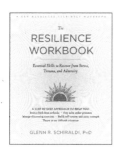

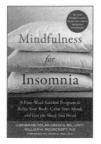

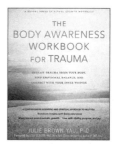

THE RESILIENCE WORKBOOK
Essential Skills to Recover from Stress, Trauma & Adversity
978-1626259409 / US $24.95

MINDFULNESS FOR INSOMNIA
A Four-Week Guided Program to Relax Your Body, Calm Your Mind & Get the Sleep You Need
978-1684032587 / US $16.95

THE BODY AWARENESS WORKBOOK FOR TRAUMA
Release Trauma from Your Body, Find Emotional Balance & Connect with Your Inner Wisdom
978-1684033256 / US $21.95

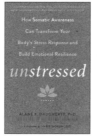

THE WORRY TRICK
How Your Brain Tricks You into Expecting the Worst & What You Can Do About It
978-1626253186 / US $17.95

UNSTRESSED
How Somatic Awareness Can Transform Your Body's Stress Response & Build Emotional Resilience
978-1684032839 / US $16.95

OUTSMART YOUR SMARTPHONE
Conscious Tech Habits for Finding Happiness, Balance & Connection IRL
978-1684033492 / US $16.95

newharbingerpublications
1-800-748-6273 / newharbinger.com

(VISA, MC, AMEX / prices subject to change without notice)
Follow Us 🄫 🔲 🔲 🔲 🔲 🔲

Don't miss out on new books in the subjects that interest you.
Sign up for our **Book Alerts** at **newharbinger.com/bookalerts**